TROUBLE DON'T
LAST ALWAYS

TROUBLE DON'T LAST ALWAYS

Emancipatory Hope among African American Adolescents

Evelyn L. Parker

THE
PILGRIM
PRESS
Cleveland

To My Parents,

Geraldine Foster Parker

and

Jesse Parker

The Pilgrim Press
700 Prospect Avenue East
Cleveland, Ohio 44115-1100
pilgrimpress.com

Scripture quotations unless otherwise noted are from the New Revised Stan-dard Version Bible, copyright © 1989 by the Division of Christian Education of the National Council of the Churches of Christ in the U.S.A., and are used by permission.

Printed in the United States of America on acid-free paper

Library of Congress Cataloging-in-Publication Data
Parker, Evelyn L., 1953-
    Trouble don't last always : emancipatory hope among African American
adolescents / Evelyn L. Parker.
        p. cm.
    Includes index.
    ISBN 0-8298-1540-6 (pbk. : alk. paper)
    1. African American youth –Religious life   I. Title.
BR563.N4P385 2003
259′.23′08996073–dc21
                                                              2003043352

CONTENTS

PREFACE

In *Black Song* John Lowell Jr. argues that the African American spiritual presented a realistic view of the slaves' present life while they expected God to deliver them to freedom. The song "I'm So Glad Trouble Don't Last Always" demonstrates the slaves' realistic response to pain, trouble, and hopelessness.[1] The poet of this spiritual wrote:

> I'm so glad trouble don't last always.
> I'm so glad trouble don't last always.
> I'm so glad trouble don't last always.
> O my Lord, O my Lord, what shall I do?

This stanza also became a popular verse in other spirituals such as "Soon One Mawnin' Death Come Creepin' in Yo' Room" and "Hush, Hush, Somebody's Callin' Mah Name." "I'm So Glad Trouble Don't Last Always" captures the assurance and hope of our African American slave ancestors and their petition to God about how they should act in times of trouble. This spiritual gives us a glimpse of the hope and courage seated at the heart of the African American slaves' spirituality. It also serves as a model of hope and courage for today's African American adolescents.

This book is about fostering a Christian spirituality in African American adolescents whereby they live holy and hope-filled lives, guided by the Spirit of God, while engaging in the challenges of social justice. Christian spirituality of this nature does two things. First, it bridges the putative chasm that divides the "spiritual" from the "physical" realities in the world.[2] Such a schism separates our holiness from our sexual, social, and political selves. All too often the perceived dualism of the spiritual and the physical is reinforced when St. Paul's directive to walk not according to the "flesh" but rather according to the "spirit" is misinterpreted as separating the spiritual from the physical. But in fact, St. Paul "urges Christians to find their motives, aspirations, and bases for action in the Holy Spirit and the things of God and not in fallen, sinful, rebellious, and self-serving attitudes that do not please God."[3] As such, Christian spirituality does not sanction movement away from the physical life, but a wedding of the physical with the spiritual.

Second, African American adolescent Christian spirituality that joins holiness with social justice produces hope among black teenagers. The Christian hope of which I speak is rooted in God made known in Jesus, who embodied hope during his ministry, who symbolizes hope as the resurrected Christ, and who brings hope in the power and presence of the Holy Spirit. This hope gives black youth the freedom to live into the fullness of their God-given potential. It is a liberating hope that paves the way for youth to flourish in all aspects of their lives.

However, Christian communities of faith are challenged to nurture black youth in such a spirituality given the social, political, and economic obstacles caused by racism, classism, and sexism in North America. These forms of oppression render many African Americans to the abyss of despair. Black children and teenagers are the most vulnerable to the hopelessness of their communities.

What is the nature of Christian spirituality that is grounded in hope while holding together piety and the politics of resisting oppression? What does Christian hope look like in the face of oppression and marginalization?

My thesis is that African American adolescent spirituality as *emancipatory hope* fosters an intricately woven life of Christian hope, holiness, and social activism against injustice. The concept of emancipatory hope means expectation that dominant powers of racism, classism, sexism, and heterosexism will be toppled and that African American adolescents have agency in God's vision for dismantling these powers of domination.

I came to the idea of emancipatory hope while pondering the results of prior research that examined a *womanist value theory*, which included Christian hope, in the life stories of urban black adolescents. The study revealed the absence of hope in the teens' life stories. Their language indicated the hopelessness, meaninglessness, and powerlessness among black youth and the black community described by Cornel West, Alvin Poussaint, Amy Alexander, and a host of other theologians, psychologists, and sociologists. At first glance, the language in the life stories revealed confidence and expectancy in areas of personal careers and professional success. A closer examination revealed language of hopelessness about race matters usually intermingled with faith language.

The teenagers I interviewed demonstrated spirituality laced with despairing sentiments of race and violence. "Racism will never end." "Drug dealing and gangbanging will never stop." "[I hope] for God to come and take us away from all this because if things go on the way they are, there's not much hope for humankind." These are some of their uncensored words juxtaposed to words that express deeply felt religious beliefs. I hope that readers will discover within the spirituality of these teens potential for Christian hope among the rubble of hopelessness. I also hope that young people themselves will open up to hope and that those who work with them will find ways to help enable Christian hope.

Although the issues of gender and sexuality are tacitly referred to in the adolescents' life stories, I do not treat these issues for two reasons. First, the youth, for the most part, did not make explicit comments on sexuality and gender during our conversations; therefore, I did not ask questions on these issues. Second, since the salient theme focuses on issues of race and racism, I attempted to stay with this theme. The youth would occasionally bring up issues of violence and death, but I discuss these issues only as they are apropos in illuminating the life stories of the youth.

I am profoundly grateful to the many people who helped me with this project. The names are so numerous that I surely will forget someone. Please forgive my forgetfulness and know I am thankful for your conversations, critiques, and words of encouragement.

This book would not have been possible had it not been for the twenty African American teenagers who gifted me with their life stories. Amid the flux of subzero temperatures, snow, and ice in Chicagoland, they made their way to previously arranged conversation rooms where the students and I explored the details of their brief histories. I am so very thankful that they trusted me with their sacred stories and held me accountable for telling them authentically.

Additionally, I owe a debt of gratitude to many others who made this project possible: to Dr. Jim Lewis and the Louisville Institute for a general grant that supported my research on Mrs. Fannie Lou Hamer; to the Association for Religion and Intellectual Life and the 1997 Collidge Fellows for insightful conversation on Hamer as one who embodied hope; to Mr. James A. Noseworthy and the Sam Taylor Fellowship Fund for support of the culminating phase of research on hopelessness in black teenagers; and to Dean Robin Lovin and Perkins School of Theology, Southern Methodist University, for providing sabbatical time for writing.

I am thankful to others who helped in a variety of ways: to Kathy Talvacchia at Union Theological Seminary in New York for reading early drafts of the conceptual framework chapter; to Charles Wood, who pushed me toward clarity of my ideas with his meticulous reading of early drafts; to John Holbert, who held me accountable for the midrash of Hebrew Bible texts; to Tom Spann, Patricia Davis, and Susanne Johnson, who encouraged me on the journey; to Ann Ralston for copyediting chapters over and over again; to Abraham Smith, who read the final draft of the entire manuscript and made invaluable suggestions for improving its readability; to Mary Elizabeth Moore for her editing and advice on the introduction and chapters 1 and 6; and to Karen Baker-Fletcher and Garth Baker-Fletcher for their support and hand-holding during the eleventh hour before sending the manuscript to my editor. Thanks to Tim Staveteig at The Pilgrim Press for guiding me through the publishing process.

Finally, thank you to my parents, Geraldine and Jesse Parker, who prayed me through the entire writing and publishing experience. At times your love and encouragement carried me when I was too tired to move ahead. You are my tangible grace from God.

Notes

1. John Lowell Jr., *Black Song* (New York: Macmillan, 1972), 293–94, 296. Lowell discusses the complexity of the African American spirituals, emphasizing the slaves' choice of the Christian faith and their appreciation of things gone awry, riddles in life, and insurmountable troubles.

2. John R. Tyson, ed., *Invitation to Christian Spirituality: An Ecumenical Anthology* (New York: Oxford University Press, 1999), 4.

3. Ibid.

INTRODUCTION

Vivid images of Jim Crow, picket lines, mass meetings, and hate crimes are etched in my memory of early adolescence as though it were yesterday.[1] These events were enough to pull most youth and their families into the abyss of hopelessness. However, my African American community, especially the church, was the womb of hope protecting its youth from despair while nurturing their expectation. Though on many occasions our bodies were vulnerable to the violence of a white supremacist mentality, our minds were saturated with idealism, expectancy, and a sense of invincibility that made us feel able to transform the world. My local congregation, parents, relatives, teachers, and neighbors nurtured hope in their teenagers, who were struggling to make sense of the evils of racism while forming a spirituality. I marvel at the ability of my congregation and its constituent churches to foster hope in its teenagers amidst the turbulent events of the time. A snapshot view of my life, an African American female, coming of age in southern Mississippi, illustrates how my community and congregation fostered hope.

In June of 1961 my mother, father, brother, and I moved away from my maternal grandmother's farm, outside of the small town of Mt. Olive, Mississippi, to the city of Hattiesburg. I was eight years old. My parents left meager salaries and dual professions of farmer and teacher for the single professions of district Boy Scout executive (my father) and teacher (my mother). Better jobs and better salaries were their expectations of the city. For me, a country girl, adjustment to city life had its ups and downs. The entertainment opportunities were the hallmark. Unlike Mt. Olive, Hattiesburg had movie theaters and many more department stores. There was the Sears and Roebuck department store, with its two water fountains. The one on the left, the dingy-dirty one, had a sign above it that read "Colored Only." The one on the right, the shiny-clean one, had a sign above it that read "White Only." I remember seeing with my parents the 1965 movie *The Sound of Music* while sitting in the balcony of the downtown Sanger Theater. We purchased our tickets in the alley at the tiny ticket booth on the side of the theater. The winding stairs took us up to a spacious area with folding wooden seats. We sat high above the crowd of white people below. I felt that we had the best seats in the house because we had a perfect view of the big screen, free of all shapes and sizes of heads blocking the view.

Walking downtown was like moving through thick air. There was always the feeling of pushing against a strong, invisible force. You could not see it. You only felt the tiredness of your muscles and the frustration of your mind after being downtown. This tiredness was relieved only when you returned across the tracks to the African American neighborhood. It sheltered us from the onerous atmosphere of downtown.

My neighbors were a blending of factory workers, cooks, maids, gardeners, and teachers. They served as Sunday school teachers, stewards and deacons, stewardesses and deaconesses in their local churches (male and female laypeople engaged in ministry), as well as public school teachers and leaders in the Civil Rights Movement (also referred to as the Movement). They were the same folks, only wearing different hats after work at the plant or the school, consistently living a theology of justice and love in the plant, the school, and the church. In contrast to downtown, in my neighborhood the air was light, electric, and pulsating with possibility.

In my neighborhood the Civil Rights Movement set the tempo for work, worship, and play. When Steelman's Grocery, a white-owned neighborhood store, would not hire black cashiers, a boycott was launched. Each day persons on the picket line carried placards and chanted demands. The boycott was a success — one of several. The African American community also launched a citywide boycott in June of 1967 under the leadership of Mr. J. C. Fairley, president of the National Association for the Advancement of Colored People (NAACP), and steward in my congregation. The boycott demanded the elimination of Jim Crow in the Sears department store, the Sanger Theater, Woolworth's five and dime, and all the businesses of the city, as well as the hiring of black bus drivers, clerks, cashiers, and in every form of employment where blacks were being denied jobs because of the color of their skin. On January 22, 1964, a group of more than 150 blacks marched to the county courthouse and tried to register to vote under the watchful eye of more than fifty Northern white clergy sponsored by the National Council of Churches.[2]

Many neighborhood churches joined in the struggle for freedom. I remember the laypeople from neighborhood churches, more than the clergy, providing the leadership for the Movement in Hattiesburg and Forrest County. They served as officers in the NAACP, the Southern Christian Leadership Conference (SCLC), and the Student Nonviolent Coordinating Committee (SNCC). Clergy at the heart of the Movement proclaimed freedom and justice from the pulpit on Sunday mornings and participated in protest marches alongside members of the congregation during the week. Even if a pastor was removed from the center of the Movement, laypeople continued midweek civil rights mass meetings in their churches.

My church, St. James Christian Methodist Episcopal (CME) Church, located on the northwest side of town, was one of those churches. In addition to Mr. Fairley, another leading steward served as president of the Forrest County NAACP. Several women served on committees and boards. More than half of the members of the St. James Christian Youth Fellowship (CYF) were active members of the Junior NAACP and had participated in freedom marches and boycotts around the state. On occasion our congregation of fewer than sixty people hosted mass meetings, with an overflow crowd standing along the walls of the sanctuary, in the choir stand, and clustered down the steps of the front door. Issues related to the Movement were heard in Sunday school, worship services, committees, boards, and auxiliary meetings. Prayers, songs, and sermons focused on the theme of hope — God making a way out of no way amidst the struggle for freedom and justice. I do not recall the explicit Sunday school curriculum focusing on justice. However, the implicit curriculum, which is the tacit socialization in the church, bathed the youth in a social theology of involvement and confident expectation. The people of the congregation saw the threads of their spiritual selves woven together with the threads of their political selves. Our spiritual identity was best described as the *social justice tradition,* rather than Evangelical, Charismatic, Afrocentric, or Holiness, using the spirituality typology of African Americans that Robert Franklin offers.[3]

The local SNCC office sat on the east corner of Mobile and Seventh Streets, just one block from my church. Between Sunday school and worship, St. James's youth occasionally visited the SNCC office. There we heard clicking typewriters and ringing phones and saw college students dashing about. Those students came from as far as New York and Ohio and as close as Greenville and Jackson, Mississippi, and they concretized the possibility of blacks and whites working together for racial justice. The college students of SNCC incarnated hope for our youth group.

Like some of St. James's youth, several youth groups from Baptist and African Methodist Episcopal congregations became involved in the Movement. During the week, at school, students talked about their church youth group activities and their memberships in SNCC and the Junior NAACP. The Catholic Youth Organization (CYO) of Holy Rosary Catholic Church accomplished the integration of involvement in the Movement with church youth group activities more than did most congregations.[4] This vibrant youth group gave its teens the license to make decisions regarding participation in boycotts and protest marches. They designed and implemented financial programs related to their activism and found time to participate in sports and other activities. CYO meetings were on Sunday night, and the more than thirty youth returned on Monday night for Junior NAACP. Adults, except for the priest, were barred from these meetings intentionally so that the teens could practice the skills of leadership. The group valued unity, using the motto "All for One and One for All," and viewed themselves as a family. Prayer also was important for the youth. CYO and Junior NAACP meetings always opened in prayer. Afterwards, youth talked about their prayers as they reflected on the activity of God and the events of the Movement. One momentous event was a decision to paint a statue of the Blessed Virgin black, which flowed out of discussion from prayers given during a youth meeting. Discussions about the Mother of God as not white and affirmation of black culture resulted in a decision to paint the Blessed Virgin black.[5] This stirred considerable controversy among some African Americans of the community. However, Father Quinn, the parish priest, supported the CYO members, who also decided to paint other statues in the church black. This youth group integrated the spirituality, activism, fellowship, leadership development, and other aspects of its sociopolitical milieu into its ministry.

The integrative aspect of ministry for St. James CYF was not as evident as that of the CYO of Holy Rosary Catholic Church. However, there were moments when St. James's youth group approximated such integration. When youth attended the CME National Youth Conferences, they heard powerful speeches on freedom and justice from the bishops and conference leaders. When I was sixteen, a decisive moment in my life was hearing my bishop, Dr. Joseph A. Johnson Jr., give the keynote address on the campus of Miles College. The title was "The Imperative of Beyondness," illuminating the conference theme, "Beyond Blackness to Destiny." In this speech thousands of CME teenagers from around the country heard words of hope regarding the African American struggle for freedom and justice. Teens from our congregation already had participated in worship and service projects with district and annual conference teens. Now we were among other youth who shared common experiences of the Movement, and its influence on our congregations was nuanced by geographical settings of east, west, north, and south.

The youth group that nurtured me was an island of hope in the middle of a sea of racist, political, and economic despair. My congregation, neighbors, teachers, and church family encouraged me, sometimes demanding that I move beyond my circumstance of hopelessness with the confidence and power to change the world. My fledgling spirituality was rooted in the belief that with God all things are possible.

The sociopolitical milieu when I was coming of age in the late 1960s is different from that of African American teenagers coming of age in the 1990s. African American communities are no longer considered as bastions against the evils of racism. Predominantly black schools, churches, and families forming our neighborhoods are no longer assumed as the respite ecology for black children. The black church is not connected with a viable movement comparable in purpose, youth involvement, and media visibility to the Civil Rights Movement.

Almost three decades later, my sixteen-year-old cousin, Jose, had a different experience growing up in Hattiesburg than I did. Jose was not confronted with segregated water fountains, schools, and theaters. The sacrifice and struggle of grassroots folks, such as Vernon Dahmer, a civil rights leader who died as a result of his house being firebombed, had transformed that aspect of apartheid. Jose attended Hattiesburg High School, now the only high school in the city. On occasion he excelled academically, particularly in math and science. However, during his junior year he dropped out of school as a result of a series of conflicts with school authorities and a lack of interest in the process of the educational system.

Jose's neighborhood, where I grew up, now shows signs of poverty and neglect. Most of the teachers from the former all-black high school and junior high school are retired but still in the neighborhood. However, for many reasons they are no longer intentional about shaping the lives of youth. The majority of young black professionals live in the suburbs.

The leaders of the Movement from St. James CME Church have retired. There is no evidence of young leadership committed to the cause of social justice emerging within the congregation. Although it once was strongly committed to social justice, it now has adopted an evangelical spirituality.[6] The values of the youth group have changed from concern for social justice, although education maintains its lofty place. The schisms among the middle class, the working class, and the very poor send strong signals of who's in and who's out. My cousin Jose, for example, comes from a poor family and never felt that the St. James congregation and youth group offered a place where he could flourish. Jose's experience significantly contrasts with my experience in the way our church and community nurtured hope. Unlike Jose and his siblings, some poor youth in the congregation during the 1960s were resilient to dehumanizing incidents of class stratification. Although Jose is from a city in southern Mississippi, in many ways his story parallels that of African American adolescents I interviewed in the Chicago area during the mid-1990s.

So what expectations do African American youth hold concerning racial injustice? What expectations do black youth hold about other issues important for them, such as violence? How relevant is the black church to the issues that circumscribe the lives of urban black youth? How is the black church instrumental in confronting racial injustice that black youth experience? What signs of hope do black youth identify as being offered by the black church? Can the church fashion black adolescent spirituality rooted in Christian hope and action? This book seeks to address these questions by considering the spiritual voices of African American adolescents coming of age during the mid-1990s in and around the city of Chicago. I offer the concept of emancipatory hope as a vital paradigm for an African American adolescent spirituality and as a theological framework for congregations concerned about fostering Christian hope in African American teenagers. Emancipatory hope means to expect transformation of hegemonic relations of race, class, and gender and to act as God's agent ushering in God's vision of human equality.

I interviewed African American adolescents from the Austin Community on the west side of Chicago and from various communities in Evanston, Illinois. The Austin Community is a predominantly black neighborhood with problems of poverty, crime, and violent gang activity. Evanston is a predominantly white middle- and upper-class suburb on the north shore of Chicago with many dense pockets of people of African descent who migrated from various neighborhoods of Chicago to Evanston. Twenty teens were interviewed. Five girls and five boys are from the Austin Community, all of whom attend Austin High School, except for one male student who attends a vanguard school for academically gifted students in Chicago. The five girls and five boys from Evanston all attend Evanston Township High School. They range in age from fifteen to eighteen years old. All acknowledge that religion is important in their lives, and all attend church with some regularity.

The research method for the collection of the life stories of the teenagers is a type of ethnography in which autobiographies are elicited using an interview protocol rich with metaphorical, open-ended questions. I do not use "life story" to mean autobiographical texts written by the adolescents, as some psychologists and sociologists use life story method. Each life story was audio-recorded and transcribed, meticulously allowing the voices of the teens to speak without embellishment. Not all of the teens use inclusive language, but I feel that it is important for you to hear their own words (more or less). These life stories serve as case studies revealing the issues of race central to the spirituality of these teens. This qualitative research shares the religious meaning-making of individuals and is not statistically valid or replicable data.[7] As such, this research is not generalizable to other populations of African American adolescents, but rather serves as a catalyst for my analysis and constructive reflections on ministry with black youth.

Chapters 1–6 are organized into three sections. Each begins with a life story of one or more teenagers. These stories describe the spirituality of the teenagers and in most cases the salient issues of race and violence. These spiritual narratives are followed by my analysis of the salient issues identified in the life story and informed by a womanist hermeneutic. Each chapter concludes with a constructive proposal to the issues resulting from analysis, couched in the theological framework of emancipatory hope. The main titles of chapters 2–6 are quotations clipped from the transcribed interviews of the teens.

Chapter 1, "Emancipatory Hope: African American Adolescent Spirituality," discusses the conceptual framework of emancipatory hope. Here social, historical, political, theological, ethical, educational, and biblical sources are orchestrated for the symphonic rendition of the idea of emancipatory hope.

Chapter 2, " 'Stop All This Racism': Fractures in Black Adolescent Spirituality," takes its title from the lead spiritual profile in the chapter. The issue of racism, generally speaking, is the focus of the chapter. The teenagers offer expressions of despair concerning the perpetual presence of racism and perceptions of God's activity in this hopeless situation. Analysis of their concerns focuses on the teens' expectations of the eternal evil of racism, their definition of racism, and analysis of language as ventriloquation of media culture (ventriloquation is speech that is mimicked from another person). Emancipatory hope explores Elisabeth Schüssler Fiorenza's term "oppositional imagination" as an aspect of black adolescent spirituality.

Chapter 3, " 'I'm Mixed': The Politics of Racial Identity," focuses on the Chicago area teens' concerns of negotiating a biracial identity, having white friends, and being the only black in academic settings. Analysis of these themes focuses on racial identity development, particularly colorism, or the prominence of skin color and its influence on racial identity development in the lives of African American adolescents. This analysis examines the dynamics of shame, honor, and self-worth regarding colorism. Emancipatory hope posits the transcendence from the "shame" of colorism to self-affirmation as an aspect of a healthy black adolescent spirituality.

Chapter 4, " 'I Don't See Color': Female Adolescent Gangs," examines girl gangs because some girls described dramatic conflicts at school between all-black groups of girls and groups with white participants. "I Don't See Color" is a metaphor that captures the girls' reflections on issues of justice in the midst of interracial relationships. Specific topics are "acting black and acting white" and being "black enough." Analysis of the conflicts between the adolescent girl gangs reveals deeper issues of black and white female relationships. Emancipatory hope explores loyalty as an aspect of spirituality among black and white adolescent girls.

Chapter 5, " 'I Face Getting Pulled Over a Lot': Racial Profiling," looks at the experiences of some of the African American male adolescents regarding racial profiling. Analysis of the teens' experiences focuses on their methods of resistance. Emancipatory hope explores moral agency as an aspect of spirituality among African American male adolescents.

Chapter 6, "'I Snapped, Man': Teenage Rage," focuses on issues of rage expressed by the teens. Some students elaborated on the anger they experienced growing up and the role their pastors and members of their congregations played in helping them cope with their anger. The youth share their experiences of violence, as participants and recipients. Also included is a discussion of death in the lives of the Chicago teens. They share their pain from the loss of family and friends, and their ways of coping. Emancipatory hope proposes the idea of "holy indignation" as an aspect of African American adolescent spirituality. Holy indignation is the freedom of young people to vent their rage in the sacred space of the congregation.

Chapter 7, "Hoping against Hope?" revisits the guiding questions and key themes in the idea of emancipatory hope explored in each chapter. An attempt is made to illustrate emancipatory hope in a practical way regarding teen and adult leadership.

In a letter to the exiles in Babylon, the young prophet Jeremiah wrote,

> For thus says the LORD:...I will fulfill to you my promise....For surely I know the plans I have for you, says the LORD, plans for your welfare and not for harm, to give you a future with hope. (Jeremiah 29:10–11)

God's words through the prophet Jeremiah are timeless. Even in these early days of the twenty-first century, communities of faith are challenged to live into God's promise of a future with hope for all its constituents: children, teenagers, and adults. And this is precisely what God requires of congregations, to incarnate God's prophetic word of a good future with hope. As such, congregations partner with God as they foster hope in all members of the community, especially those who bear the future of the community: children and youth.

Notes

1. I use Shirley Feldman and Glenn Elliott's definitions of early adolescence (ages ten to fourteen), middle adolescence (ages fifteen to seventeen), and late adolescence (eighteen to midtwenties), in *At the Threshold* (Cambridge, Mass.: Harvard University Press, 1990).

2. See Clayborne Carson, *In Struggle: SNCC and the Black Awakening of the 1960s* (Cambridge, Mass.: Harvard University Press, 1981).

3. See Robert M. Franklin, *Another Day's Journey: Black Churches Confronting the American Crisis* (Minneapolis: Fortress Press, 1997).

4. Interview with Father Peter Quinn, parish pastor at Holy Rosary Catholic Church, September 2000.

5. Ibid.

6. See Franklin, *Another Day's Journey.*

7. See Patricia H. Davis, *Beyond Nice: The Spiritual Wisdom of Adolescent Girls* (Minneapolis: Fortress Press, 2000).

CHAPTER ONE

EMANCIPATORY HOPE

African American Adolescent Spirituality

Emancipatory hope is expectation that the forms of hegemonic relations —race, class, and gender dominance —will be toppled, and to have
emancipatory hope is to acknowledge one's personal agency in God's
vision for human equality. This is the theological framework that guides
my constructive response to issues of skepticism, cynicism, and despair
that are themes in the life stories of twenty African American teenagers.
Hopelessness enshrouds the spirituality of these teens.

To begin the discourse on emancipatory hope, I offer the spiritual profile of Lisa. I do not intend to suggest solutions to Lisa's hopelessness,
but to use her story to illustrate the problem of hopelessness, followed
by a systematic conceptualization of emancipatory hope. Although Lisa
believes strongly in God's salvific power, she does not connect salvation
with the expectation that the troubles of the world, troubles that she
identifies, will be transformed. Her language evinces wishful thinking. I
argue that wishful thinking is not hope, and I offer an understanding of
Christian hope that is liberative and efficacious.

Salvation and Wishful Thinking:
Lisa's Story

Lisa is a seventeen-year-old senior at Evanston Township High School.
She has been accepted into several universities and looks forward to
college life following graduation from high school. She lives with her
mother, father, and younger brother. They are an upper-middle-class
family, with an annual income of more than $100,000. She is thank-
ful that her "parents have always done everything that [she and her]
brother have wanted." Communication between Lisa, her brother, and
her parents has been central to their relationship. As far back as she can

remember, "Religion has always been important to the household." Lisa and her family are active participants in the Baptist congregation where they are members. Her contribution of an original liturgical dance to a church play produced and performed by the choir offered a moment of exhilaration in church life for Lisa. She recalls,

> I wasn't sure how to go about doing the moves because...I was performing for my church, and you know, it was spiritual music and you're not supposed to really dance to stuff like that. It was a hard task for me; it took me about four weeks to really come down to the basic steps. But it was fun. I really enjoyed doing it because I felt joy presenting it to other people....I gave something important....When I dance, everything else seems to be locked out, and I'm focused on that. And I feel good about myself when I do things like that, and to do it for my church made me feel really good.

Lisa has not always felt good about her religious experiences. One example was the pressure she experienced from her family to commit publicly her life to God, to "get saved." After her brother "got saved," her parents began to ask, "Why don't [you] think about it?" She explained,

> And they were comparing me to him....And that made me feel bad because I was being compared to someone else as far as religion goes, and it's not something that you can just tell a person to do...and expect them to do it. It's something that they have to do for themselves. And I was trying to explain that to them, and they'd come back with something else, you know.

The discussion regarding getting saved continued between Lisa and her parents. She admits that in addition to making her feel "really bad," it made her "think about it a whole lot more" than before. Lisa was not sure she was prepared to give up the many things that "saved people" must reject, such as listening to "rap music, dancing and attending parties." Being saved, for Lisa, means "being into the Bible...following the rules...attending church regularly, which I already do," said Lisa, and acting in ways "that people will know you are a religious person."

Although Lisa and her family have struggled over the day she will become saved, her cousins occasionally have eased that tension. One joyous occasion was when her cousins took her to a gospel concert. Lisa said, "I had a great time....It really put me in good spirits....They were like, um, I guess you would say a ministry as well as singing, you know, and it helped me see a lot of things differently, it put new ideas in my head. It gave me hope; it put me back in high spirit." Lisa continued to explain what she meant by the concert giving her hope:

> I had discussed with my parents about being saved. And it's something that I haven't done yet because I'm scared of the change that I think it will bring to my life, the age I am. Not being able to do what I used to do and things like that. And I realized that there were a lot of people in the same predicament that I was that night, and they knew that they should be saved.

Lisa is very close to her cousins, so much so that it was almost unbearable when two of them, brothers ages twenty-one and twenty-two, died from a rare heart condition. Two months later Lisa lost her grandmother, who had suffered from diabetes. Lisa said,

> My aunts and uncles came out from North Carolina to see her before she passed, and I kept saying to myself, "She's not going to die, she's not going to die, she can't. She's been through all of this so far [her grandsons' deaths]; you know God won't let her go yet." And he did. And it upset me at first because I was wondering why, why he had let this happen; but I had to deal with it.

Lisa integrates her religious beliefs into many aspects of her life. Religious beliefs and commitments, as well as family, are intertwined. She does not hesitate to express disappointment in family and God while still expressing her love for them. Salvation is the theological motif woven throughout Lisa's life story. Her understanding of being saved is God's power to transform and convert one's life.

Although Lisa eagerly expressed her beliefs about salvation, her tenor changed when she talked about other aspects of hope. When I asked her to talk about her hopes for humankind, Lisa responded,

> I always used to see a fountain and throw a quarter into it. [I'd] make a wish that, please make the world better. [If] all bad things can be prevented, it would be different if it could be something that can be helped, but it can't be.

Even though Lisa has strong religious convictions about her personal salvation, faithfully attends church each week with her family, and is an active participant in the church youth group and drama ministry, she does not apply her spirituality to the transformation of hopeless situations with which she is concerned. Lisa jettisoned the religious language she demonstrated in sharing her beliefs about salvation and replaced it with "wish" language — the evidence of wishful thinking. This type of language juxtaposed to language about salvation raises questions about the presence of Christian hope in Lisa's repertoire of beliefs.

Lisa demonstrated a better example of wishful thinking than any of the other teenagers who also used "wish" language. Like Lisa, four youth discussed in chapter 2 — Daryl, Betty, Kathy, Paul — also demonstrate wishful thinking about their most troubling concerns. These youth talked of their hopes either using wish language or expressing a tone of desire and longing. Sometimes their hopes were pitched in an incredulous tone that leads one to conclude that there is little or no expectation for their wishes to come true.

The Problem of Wishful Thinking

For Lisa and several other youth interviewed, to hope means to wish. It's a desire and a longing void of possibility and personal agency. The act of wishing lacks potential for the realization of that for which one wishes. Wishing is associated with fantasy, the magical, the fairy tale, and the dreamy. Hope, on the other hand, is associated with expectancy, confidence, assurance, and faith.

At best, wishing represents the germinal element of expectation of a good future. Metaphorically speaking, it is the seed of hope. Wishing comprises the rudiments of dreams. Though essentially important, wishing is not synonymous with hope. "Hoping has a possibility condition that wishing does not have."[1] Hoping is related to "action or dispositions to act" not afforded those who wish.[2] The person who hopes disposes herself to act as if that for which she hopes is realizable, obtainable, and true.

This book proposes an alternative to the problem of wishful thinking or the act of wishing demonstrated in Lisa and several of the teens interviewed. I offer emancipatory hope as a theological framework for congregations that are intentional about fostering hope in African American teenagers through ministry with them.

Emancipatory Hope

To possess emancipatory hope is to expect transformation of hegemonic relations and to act as God's agent ushering in God's vision of equality for humankind.[3] "Emancipatory" means freedom from domination.[4] Verbs such as "challenge," "examine," "confront," "free," and "transform" are commonly used in association with the term "emancipatory." To possess emancipatory hope is to expect that hegemonic relations will be transformed and to acknowledge personal agency in God's vision for human equality. It can be illustrated by movements that seek freedom from domination.

There have been many movements of freedom from domination, beginning with the ancient period. The Jesus Movement, argues Elisabeth Schüssler Fiorenza, was an emancipatory movement subverting the kyriarchal structures of domination and exploitation and reconstructing an egalitarian model with the "*basileia* (empire/commonweal) of G*d" as its guiding metaphor.[5] During the 1400s Joan of Arc, a young woman about seventeen years old, received divine orders from Saints Catherine and Margaret and the archangel Michael to break the siege of Orleans during the Hundred Years' War (1337–1453) and deliver the dauphin to Rheims for crowning as Charles VII. Although her emancipatory movement was successful, "she was accused of heresy for claiming to receive orders from heaven, for insisting that these orders were given in French, and for dressing as a man."[6] After signing a recantation and receiving a sentence of life in prison, she again claimed visions from heaven, and subsequently she was burned alive in 1431, at about twenty years of age.[7] Sojourner Truth, an undaunted prophetic itinerant preacher, abolitionist, and champion of women's rights during the 1800s, sought freedom from domination on behalf of oppressed women and blacks. She was in solidarity with other women of her era who sought women's rights. Truth's renowned "Ain't I a Woman?" speech delivered in Akron, Ohio, on May 29, 1851, spoke against male dominance and also critiqued class and racial biases among white female suffragists and their rhetoric on "True Womanhood."[8] Sojourner Truth was a transformative leader in the emancipatory movements of women's suffrage and black freedom. Not only an essential protagonist in these emancipatory movements, she was an exemplar of hope for people of African descent and for the whole North American Christian community.

Hope is decidedly Christian and rooted in the experiences and beliefs of African American women, children, and men. It is expectation of deliverance from economic, political, and racial oppression through the power of God, which requires one to live in the present as an agent of change for God's justice. James Cone discusses hope from the perspective of black liberation theology. He states, "Black religion as its emphasis on hope came into being through black people's encounter with the Crucified and Risen Lord in the context of American slavery."[9] The songs, prayers, sermons, and stories of African American slaves reveal such a hope. The slaves would sing in the words of the spiritual, *Oh, freedom! Oh, freedom! Oh, freedom all over me! An' befo' I'd be a slave, I'll be buried in my grave, An' go home to my Lord an' be free.* The words indicate expectation of freedom from the dehumanizing institution of slavery. Slaves sang about the certainty of God's power for deliverance from slavery, and then supported this claim with biblical evidence. Another example is the spiritual "Didn't My Lord Deliver Daniel?" The slave professed in colorful imagery what Joan Martin calls an "apocalyptic eschatology,"[10] expressing hope in the end of history, impending judgment, and permanent arrival in Canaan:

> *Didn't my Lord deliver Daniel, d'liver Daniel, d'liver Daniel? . . . And why not-a every man?*
>
> *He deliver'd Daniel from the lion's den, Jonah from the belly of the whale, And the Hebrew children from the fiery furnace, And why not every man?*
>
> *The moon run down in a purple stream, The sun forbear to shine, And every star disappear, King Jesus shall be mine.*
>
> *The wind blows east, and the wind blows west, It blows like the judgment day, And every poor soul that never did pray, 'll be glad to pray that day.*
>
> *I set my foot on the Gospel ship, And the ship it begin to sail, It landed me over on Canaan's shore, And I'll never come back any more.*[11]

This spiritual and others, including *Git on Board, Little Children* and *I've Got a Robe,* imply the otherworldly hope of the black slave. However, the otherworldly language sometimes was coded language signifying freedom on earth by means of the Underground Railroad rather than freedom in heaven. James Cone has critiqued this otherworldly ethos as still prevalent in black churches today.[12] This has implications for black teens socialized in congregations that promote an otherworldly ethos.

Teens who embrace the otherworldly apocalyptic or dispensational beliefs usually are pessimistic and negative about the present and see the world ending before earthly dehumanizing conditions are transformed.[13] Apocalyptic thinking in African American adolescents is a central motif in the teens' life stories that I present and later discuss more comprehensively.

Hope, on the other hand, is a verb creating active expectation of the coming presence of Jesus and requiring individuals "to live as if the vision is already realized in the present."[14]

Central to my understanding of Christian hope is the meaning of the reign, or kingdom, of God, which must be connected to emancipatory hope. Jesus taught his disciples to pray, "Father, hallowed be your name. Your kingdom come" (Luke 11:2). Here Jesus emphasizes the "highest priority of what we should hope for."[15] Gayraud Wilmore observes, "The Kingdom of God is mixed up in the real world as a partial and unfulfilled potential of its being."[16] Using the metaphor of playing cards, Wilmore continues:

> Christian hope refuses ... [to make] the present look like the future by counterfeit or, in imitation of a skillful card shark, substituting what is on the table with a marked deck. Christian hope peers into the mystery of the future with expectation and deals the cards that are already there, with the assurance that a winning combination, though difficult to come by, is somewhere in our hands.[17]

Christian hope moves within the morass of life, confronting the state of what is because of the expectation of what will be. The reign of God is in the midst of the morass of life, and at the same time is a transforming and liberating divine force. To profess an emancipatory hope and a relevant ministry with black youth requires that one "claim the liberating and sustaining power of God — the reign (kingdom) of God in Jesus Christ — as a support in our [African American] struggle against forms of oppression."[18]

Emancipatory hope pursues personal and communal freedom and agency in transforming economic, political, and racial oppression in the global society. The life and work of Fannie Lou Hamer, one who I believe embodied emancipatory hope, is a viable resource for understanding this idea. She gave witness of her expectation of freedom for all humankind in her work as a civil rights activist from the early 1950s until her death in 1977. The legendary phase of her life began in August 1962, when she attended a mass meeting in her hometown of Ruleville, Mississippi. She heard James Forman of SNCC and James Bevel of SCLC emphasize the importance of voting. Inspired by their speeches, Hamer volunteered to go with seventeen others to the county courthouse in Indianola, Mississippi, to register to vote. She was selected as the leader for the group seeking to obtain full U.S. citizenship as registered voters. After three attempts, Hamer succeeded and became a registered voter in Sunflower County.

The status of being a registered voter marked the beginning of threats to the lives of Hamer and her family and her unceasing commitment to the civil rights struggle. As an organizer she helped to found the Mississippi Freedom Democratic Party (MFDP), which opened its office in May 1964. During the 1964 Democratic Convention, Hamer led the MFDP in a heated debate with leaders of the Democratic Party regarding seating of the MFDP delegation. The Democratic Party offered only two seats for the MFDP delegation instead of seating all its delegates. Under Hamer's leadership the MFDP rejected the compromise, and none of its delegates were seated.[19] In 1968, the MFDP changed its name to Mississippi Loyalist Democratic Party (MLDP). Once again, MLDP challenged the credentials committee of the Democratic Convention, demanding to be seated as regular delegates. This time they were victorious. Hamer was the first black woman to run for Congress from the Second District of Mississippi.

In 1970, Hamer shifted her energies to focus on the war on poverty. She organized the Freedom Farm Co-operative, where she obtained from 40 to 640 acres of land provided for poor families to build homes and raise crops for food. The Freedom Farm Co-operative provided homes for black and white families in poverty-ridden Sunflower County, Mississippi. She later founded the Ruleville garment factory and a day care center for children of working parents.

Amid the ominous realities of Southern apartheid, Hamer held the Christian conviction of hope in God, whose presence through the power of the Holy Spirit helps one confront lethal acts of racism. Like a modern-day prophet, Hamer seldom hesitated to offer prophetic critique of local, state, and national public officials. In a letter to Rose Fishman in Massachusetts, Hamer wrote,

> Two FBI [men] came to check with me. They had got the report from Ralph about the five of us on the list to be killed but I told them to solve some of [the] murders that had already been committed

and nothing was being done about that. If they keep dragging the Mississippi River and Pearl River and the Tallachachie River they will be shocked when they find some of the cruel things that has been going on across the years to people. And if it hadn't been two whites with that one Negro nothing would have been done.[20]

On an earlier occasion, days after Hamer had been beaten severely in a jail in Winona, Mississippi, she confronted the jailer as he escorted her to the trial, saying, "Do you people ever think or wonder how you'll feel when the time comes you'll have to meet God?"[21] She knew how to use her words to cut like a two-edged sword, simultaneously convicting and raising consciousness.

Hamer's convictions were articulated in her speeches, letters, and, most powerfully, in her singing at organizational meetings and during marches. She would sing "I want Jesus to walk with me," invoking the presence of Jesus before and during protest marches. Likewise, she sang "Precious Lord, take my hand, lead me on, let me stand," entreating God's "felt" presence when facing racist and sexist Mississippi public officials.

Hamer inspired students in Nashville, including Jim Lewis, by sharing her story and her hopes.[22] Unita Blackwell recalled Hamer's belief: "You have to love 'em. . . . America was sick and it needed a doctor and we was the hope of America."[23]

Hamer's socioeconomic and political milieu was different from that of black urban youth of the 90s. She could see her oppressors face to face. Urban youth may never see the face of their oppressors.[24] Nevertheless, her life bears witness to the capacity of emancipatory hope to transcend the circumstances caused by one's socioeconomic and political context, specifically those circumstances of race, class, and gender dominance. To have emancipatory hope is to expect that these forms of hegemonic relations will be toppled and to acknowledge one's personal agency in God's vision of human equality.

Epistemology and Spirituality

Emancipatory hope calls attention to two interrelated areas of concern regarding the lives of African American adolescents: epistemology and spirituality. Although I view epistemology as an aspect of one's spirituality, I will discuss the two separately and then reintegrate them in subsequent analysis.

Epistemology

By "epistemology," I mean a way of knowing, whereby an African American adolescent makes sense of and creates meaning from his or her experiences. Creating meaning involves the cognitive processes of discerning, thinking, comprehending, and understanding, as well as the affective processes of coherence, discovery, and possibility.[25] Epistemology is related to issues of ideology that influence identity formation in African American adolescents.[26] The combination of social history, "ideologically driven activities available in the community and larger society, as well as the day-to-day character of the infrastructure for families" provides the resources for ideology and identity formation in late adolescence or early adulthood.[27]

The process of meaning-making in African American adolescents is sabotaged by the ideological hegemony of racism, sexism, and classism. Black youth must find ways to subvert these oppressive forms of ideology. Just as black women assert their unique consciousness amid continuous struggle for survival against "ideological hegemony of racism, sexism, and class privilege,"[28] so too must black youth dismantle ideological domination within their thoughts and consciousnesses. Ministry with black youth must free them from the ideology that demands conformity, that stratifies and classifies based on standards set by the dominant culture. Black youth must construct knowledge — create meaning — as they confront oppressive dominance in the global society. Ministry focusing upon emancipatory hope fosters thought and consciousness that is imaginative, creative, and critical. It helps black youth deconstruct hegemony and reconstruct models of justice and equality in their immediate context and in the global society. Emancipatory hope fosters new ways of meaning-making in black youth victimized by an oppressive dominant culture. Youth set free by emancipatory hope envision an alternative world free of "political, economic, racial and cultural injustice."[29] Educational ministry for emancipatory hope is one form of ministry with black youth that illustrates my point.

Educator Beverly Gordon of Ohio State University has influenced my ideas on educational ministry for emancipatory hope. In her essay

"Toward Emancipation in Citizenship Education: The Case of African-American Cultural Knowledge," Gordon probes the basic notion of citizenship education in the United States, targeting the role of schools designed to promote an ideological hegemony that legitimates and reproduces a society replete with inequities of wealth and power. She states,

> The question is whether we, as educators, intend education for citizenship simply to function as a mode of ideological domination, conforming students to the demands of dominant society; or whether citizenship education should be designed to foster social reconstruction, by helping students (and others) to become creative, critical thinkers and active social participants, and to become capable of redefining the nature of their own lives in the society in which they live.[30]

Gordon suggests that our primary educational task is "to determine how it is that citizenship education functions to reproduce the social condition of labor and the mechanisms of social control that reinforce a class-stratified society; or, alternatively, how citizenship education can be designed to equip students to challenge and reconstitute society according to the principles of social justice and equitable economic opportunity."[31]

Gordon's solution is emancipatory pedagogy, whereby students are taught civic courage and are encouraged to critique the existing society "against its own claims about its own values and what it claims to have achieved."[32] Students also are "encouraged to reconceptualize, dream, and envision different societal arrangements and possibilities."[33] Together, students and teachers experience a creatively restructured mode of relating, resulting in heightened social consciousness and mutual willingness to explore the contradictions and the struggles that occur within their daily lives.

Gordon's proposal for "emancipatory citizenship education" falls within the educational tradition of critical pedagogy or liberation education. She references the work of Henry Giroux on the three modes of rationality to structure and support her argument.[34] The first mode of rationality is "technical rationality," which is based on the "principles of prediction and control" and employs a singular view of knowledge that mistakenly claims to be value free. The second mode of rationality, "hermeneutic rationality," is concerned about understanding how "the forms, categories and assumptions beneath the texture of everyday life" contribute to our knowledge of self, our communities, and the world around us. The third mode of rationality, "emancipatory rationality," is concerned about critique and action. From Giroux's theories of technical rationality, hermeneutic rationality, and emancipatory rationality, she chooses the last. Gordon and Giroux stand in solidarity with other educators who promote liberation education, starting with Paulo Freire, and his classic book, *Pedagogy of the Oppressed.*

Emancipatory hope nurtures the gift of idealism in black youth whereby they imagine, dream, foresee, conceive the possible and the perfect as they criticize perceived hypocrisy in adults. God's gift of idealism comes at the time when adolescents develop the cognitive ability for formal operational thinking. The process of moving away from concrete to abstract thinking begins during early adolescence. Youth in middle adolescence are more proficient at abstract thinking. They think about thinking. Youthful idealism is, perhaps, God's creative process, God's imagination, if you will, evident in humankind.

Spirituality

Emancipatory hope also fosters a potent spirituality in African American adolescents.[35] A potent spirituality helps black teens critically reflect on the problem of evil and fortifies them with coping skills in the face of tragedy and disappointment. This type of spirituality is the result of belief in God's promise to always be present and spiritual disciplines that fortify black teens in good times and bad times. Emancipatory hope cultivates a spirituality in black youth whereby spiritual disciplines and Christian beliefs are intricately woven together with practices of social justice. This type of spirituality manifests itself in a seamless life of divine and human activity against economic, political, and racial dominance.

Once again, the life of Fannie Lou Hamer helps to illustrate this idea. Her life reveals a belief in God's ability to transform society, and her actions demonstrate her beliefs in a holistic way. Hamer is fondly remembered by biographers and Mississippians who knew her for her famous mantra "sick and tired of being sick and tired." She often used this phrase to express her state of weariness or exhaustion in light of dehumanization

she experienced as a poor black woman. She was not only tired personally, but also tired for the whole black community as it struggled against
race and class oppression. Her weariness moved her toward activism during the Civil Rights Movement. Kay Mills records two events in which
Hamer expressed her tiredness and that of the black community. In the
first experience, Mills quotes Jerry DeMuth, a writer for *The Nation,* report-
ing on Hamer's campaign for the U.S. Congress against Jamie Whitten,
who for twenty years was a powerful Mississippi politician in the House of
Representatives. DeMuth visited Hamer in her small wood frame house
surrounded by butter bean and okra plants in the garden and a large
pecan tree in the front of the house. Mills quotes DeMuth:

> "Her deep powerful voice shakes the air as she sits on the porch
> or inside, talking to friends, relatives and neighbors who drop by
> on the one day each week when she is not out campaigning,"
> DeMuth wrote. "Whatever she is talking about soon becomes an
> impassioned plea for a change in the system that exploits the Delta
> Negroes. 'All my life I've been sick and tired,' she shakes her head.
> 'Now I'm sick and tired of being sick and tired.' "[36]

Of another occasion, after Hamer was elected as the Second District's
representative on the MFDP executive committee, Mills writes,

> "She stood and in her booming voice spoke briefly on her theme:
> 'We are sick and tired of being sick and tired!' She told of the time
> they had shot at her, and 'my house was so full of holes it wouldn't
> hold water.' "[37]

Hamer was a devout Christian who practiced spiritual disciplines of
prayer, singing, and social action for justice. As such her life was a
weaving together of Christian piety and social activism. Hamer's life
demonstrates the spirituality characteristic of emancipatory hope.

The African American adolescent spirituality that I am trying to describe is akin to the spirituality that Emilie Townes defines as social
witness. Regarding womanist spirituality, which represents those black
feminists among the ancestral cloud of witnesses and modern-day saints,
she writes,

> Womanist spirituality is not grounded in the notion that spiritu-
> ality is a force, a practice separate from who we are moment by

moment. It is the deep kneading of humanity and divinity into one breath, one hope, one vision. Womanist spirituality is not only a way of living, it is a style of witness that seeks to cross the yawning chasm of hatreds and prejudices and oppressions into a deep and richer love of God as we experience Jesus in our lives. This love extends to self and to others. It holds together the individual and the community in a soulful relationship that cannot dwell more on one than the other partner of the relation but holds both in the same frame.[38]

Metaphorically, African American adolescent spirituality is a *kente* cloth of Ghana,[39] with brilliant threads of poetry, prose, prance, praise, petition, protest, all of who black adolescents are, human and divine, woven together. Allow me to develop this metaphor through the embellishment of this twelfth-century African ceremonial cloth with Christian symbols. In my Christian womanist liberationist imagination, black is the prominent thread in the *kente* cloth, representing a spirituality rooted in black Christianity as "an activist religion, one that emphasized being 'doers,' 'movers,' and 'shakers' for social change."[40] Such a spirituality embraces a belief in God, known in Jesus Christ and present in the world as the Holy Spirit, acting for justice so that all of humankind may flourish. Red represents political struggle, sometimes unto death; green strands are for fertility and vitality; yellow threads are for the glory of kings; gold is for life; and blue is for love and the honor of queens.[41] Purple is the thread of ancestral social witness. My implication here is that African American adolescent spirituality has the potential for social witness, regardless of its rudimentary form, because of black adolescents' four-hundred-year-old heritage in North America. Social witness gives evidence of the usefulness of the *kente* cloth, not only for its beauty for observation, but also for its ability to adorn, cover, and protect. Thus, the *kente* cloth of African American adolescent spirituality is dynamic, evolving in its brilliance as well as its utility.

In addition to the ancestral nature for social witness that African American adolescent spirituality has, such spirituality gives testimony to the presence of the "triune God,"[42] "who promises to be present in the midst of suffering and despair,"[43] joy and praise. Testimony of the triune God present during times of suffering was exemplified in the life of Fannie Lou Hamer.

Biblical witness of God's "promise never to leave us regardless of the circumstance, to be present with us even during the worst of times" is demonstrated in the Genesis story of Joseph.[44] Here I offer a slightly modified midrash on Joseph's saga from an earlier publication of mine, "Hope as a Theological Framework for Youth Ministry."

> When Joseph's brothers sold him to the Ishmaelites he no doubt felt betrayed, abandoned and afraid. Seventeen-year-old Joseph knew that his older brothers had grown to hate him because he was their father's favorite son. Joseph didn't help the sibling rivalry when he shared his "arrogant" dreams and adorned himself in that "long-sleeved" coat his father Jacob had given him. But had their jealousy and rage come to this? They were his brothers, those with whom he played and worked, yet they discarded him like a slave for twenty pieces of silver. Joseph must have cried the entire journey to Egypt, wondering if he would ever see his family again. Perhaps the memories of his father's "doting" love eased his pain. Perhaps the stories of Yahweh's presence with his father Jacob, his grandfather Isaac, and his great grandfather Abraham when they were strangers in foreign lands restored his confidence. Perhaps Joseph experienced the assurance that Yahweh was with him. Once in Egypt Potiphar, Pharaoh's captain of the guard, purchased Joseph. "The Lord was with Joseph and he prospered, and he lived in the house of his Egyptian master." (Genesis 39:2)[45]

Also, Mary the mother of Jesus, a teenage girl from Nazareth, in her joy gave testimony in song of God's favor on a girl marginalized because of her class and gender. She sings, "For [God] has looked with favor on the lowliness of his servant. Surely, from now on all generations will call me blessed; for the Mighty One has done great things for me" (Luke 1:48–49). Her testimony continues with her account of God's subversion of the politically and economically powerful on behalf of the poor: "He has brought down the powerful from their thrones, and lifted up the lowly; he has filled the hungry with good things, and sent the rich away empty" (Luke 1:52–53). Mary concludes by recalling the promise of God of which she is heir: "He has helped his servant Israel, in remembrance of his mercy, according to the promise he made to our ancestors, to Abraham and to his descendants forever" (Luke 1:54–55). Mary gives testimony of God's presence and promise in the midst of her joy and praise.

Emancipatory hope proposes a spirituality in African American adolescents that is as equally political as it is pious. The ancestors demonstrate the woven quality of the type of Christian spirituality that
emancipatory hope generates. Christian belief and social action are central to the ancestral ways of knowing. Such spirituality reveals itself as an
intricately woven life, seamless in its activity to praise God and protest
injustice. Emancipatory hope fosters an intricately woven life of both
pious and political living, where critical consciousness and critical action
sit at the core of a way of knowing, a way of meaning-making.

When Does Hope Seem Hopeless?

Racism is an important issue for the African American adolescents who
shared their stories with me. They see this dominance of evil as insurmountable for church and society. They can only wish for the end of
racism but believe that humankind ultimately will cease to exist and Jesus
will return before racism is dismantled. They feel that God is not acting
on behalf of those who struggle for justice. The church is not relevant to
the issues that circumscribe the lives of urban black teenagers. Therefore,
hope seems hopeless for African American adolescents confronted with
the realities of racism and violence in the places where they live.

Lisa's story evinces wishing as her understanding of Christian hope.
Wishful thinking is far from the hope that I propose in this book. Emancipatory hope offers personal agency in partnership with God and the
conviction that God will end unjust powers of domination.

In the next chapter I introduce several African American adolescents
who express hopelessness about racism; yet these sentiments are unattached to their strong religious beliefs. I share their spiritual stories,
give my analysis of key themes, and offer my constructive proposal in
light of *emancipatory hope.*

Notes

1. James L. Muyskens, "The Apologetic Force of a Theology of Hope," *Scottish Journal of Theology* 33, no. 2 (1980): 103.
2. Ibid.
3. I am influenced by a number of feminist and womanist writers who use the term "emancipatory." These include Elisabeth Schüssler Fiorenza, "To Follow the Vision: The Jesus Movement as Basileia Movement," in *Liberating Eschatology:*

Essays in Honor of Letty M. Russell, ed. Margaret A. Farley and Serene Jones (Louisville: Westminster John Knox Press, 1999), 123–41; Marjorie Procter-Smith, *In Her Own Rite: Constructing Feminist Liturgical Tradition* (Nashville: Abingdon Press, 1990), 59–84; 116–35; Katie Geneva Cannon, "Emancipatory Historiography," in *Dictionary of Feminist Theologies,* ed. Letty M. Russell and J. Shannon Clarkson (Louisville: Westminster John Knox Press, 1996), 81.

4. Beverly M. Gordon, "Toward Emancipation in Citizenship Education: The Case of African-American Cultural Knowledge," *Theory and Research in Social Education* 12, no. 4 (winter 1985): 1–23.

5. Schüssler Fiorenza, "To Follow the Vision," 132–37.

6. Justo L. Gonzalez, *The Story of Christianity* (San Francisco: Harper & Row, 1984), 237.

7. Regine Pernoud discusses the approximation of Joan's age in the chapter "Origins and Childhood," in *Joan of Arc* (New York: Scarborough House, 1994).

8. See Barbara Hilkert Andolsen, *Daughters of Jefferson, Daughters of Bootblacks: Racism and American Feminism* (Macon, Ga.: Mercer University Press, 1986).

9. James Cone, *God of the Oppressed,* rev. ed. (Maryknoll, N.Y.: Orbis Books, 1997), 129.

10. Joan M. Martin, "A Sacred Hope and Social Goal," in Farley and Jones, eds., *Liberating Eschatology,* 209–26.

11. "Didn't My Lord Deliver Daniel?" in *Songs of Zion,* Supplemental Worship Resources 12 (Nashville: Abingdon Press 1981), no. 106.

12. See James Cone, *Black Theology and Black Power* (1969; reprint, Maryknoll, N.Y.: Orbis Books, 1997).

13. African American beliefs concerning apocalypticism, dispensationalism, and millennialism are discussed extensively in Gayraud S. Wilmore, *Last Things First* (Philadelphia: Westminster Press, 1982).

14. Cone, *God of the Oppressed,* 129.

15. Wilmore, *Last Things First,* 54.

16. Ibid., 5.

17. Ibid.

18. Martin, "Sacred Hope and Social Goal," 210.

19. Kay Mills, *This Little Light of Mine: The Life of Fannie Lou Hamer* (New York: Penguin Books, 1993), 125–30.

20. Fannie Lou Hamer, letter to Ralph and Rose Fishman (The Fannie Lou Hamer Archives).

21. Charles Marsh, *God's Long Summer: Stories of Faith and Civil Rights* (Princeton, N.J.: Princeton University Press, 1997), 23.

22. Mills, *This Little Light of Mine,* 44.

23. Ibid., 17.

24. David Gerwin, Coolidge Fellow, 14th Association of Religion and Intellectual Life (ARIL) Research Colloquium, discussion, July 1997.

25. See Charles R. Foster, *Educating Congregations: The Future of Christian Education* (Nashville: Abingdon Press, 1994).

26. See James Garbarino, "Enhancing Adolescent Development Through Social Policy," in *Handbook of Clinical Research and Practice with Adolescents,* ed. Patrick H. Tolan and Bertram J. Cohler (New York: John Wiley and Sons, 1993), 480–81.

27. Ibid., 481.

28. Katie Cannon, "The Emergence of Black Feminist Consciousness," in *Katie's Canon: Womanism and the Soul of the Black Community* (New York: Continuum, 1995), 55.

29. Schüssler Fiorenza, "To Follow the Vision," 135.

30. Gordon, "Toward Emancipation in Citizenship Education," 2.

31. Ibid.

32. Ibid, 5.

33. Ibid.

34. Ibid., 2–3.

35. See Evelyn L. Parker, "Hope as a Theological Framework for Youth Ministry," in *Starting Right: Thinking Theologically about Youth Ministry,* ed. Kenda Creasy Dean, Chap Clark, and David Rahn (Grand Rapids: Zondervan, 2001), 270–71.

36. Mills, *This Little Light of Mine,* 93.

37. Ibid., 108.

38. Emilie M. Townes, *In a Blaze of Glory: Womanist Spirituality as Social Witness* (Nashville: Abingdon Press, 1995), 11.

39. See Sharne Algotsson and Denys Davis, *The Spirit of African Design* (New York: Clarkson Potter, 1996).

40. Joyce A. Ladner, *The Ties That Bind: Timeless Values for African American Families* (New York: John Wiley and Sons, 1998), 73.

41. Algotsson and Davis, *The Spirit of African Design,* 15, 36. Here I adapt Algotsson and Davis's description of *kente* cloth of Ghana as my metaphor to describe African American adolescent spirituality.

42. The term "triune God" is borrowed from Daniel Migliore to capture the Trinitarian nature of God, traditionally understood as God the Father, God the Son, and God the Holy Spirit. Migliore discusses the triune God in *Faith Seeking Understanding: An Introduction to Christian Theology* (Grand Rapids: Eerdmans, 1991), 60–64.

43. Parker, "Hope as a Theological Framework," 270.

44. Ibid. This midrash is a slight modification of one first printed in the essay "Hope as a Theological Framework for Youth Ministry" (n. 35 above).

45. Ibid., 270–71.

CHAPTER TWO

"STOP ALL THIS RACISM"
Fractures in Black Adolescent Spirituality

Racism is the locus of hopelessness in the lives of the urban youth I interviewed. Although many aspects of their lives seem progressive and filled with promise, concerns about racism in society and personal racist encounters consistently influenced the tenor of their conversations. Surprisingly, the teens most active in worship, Sunday school, and youth groups, and most articulate about their Christian beliefs and practices were the ones who poignantly talked about racism never ending. They offered a spectrum of thoughts ranging from nihilism, graphically displayed in language of despair, to fragments of hope, veiled in language of pessimism and cynicism. In fact, these youth juxtaposed nihilistic secular language and New Testament apocalyptic language. Absent from their conversations was the expectation that God can transform racist people and oppressive institutions of domination. Their agency to dismantle racism also was absent. Even though theological themes of God's protective presence and God's power to transform and save permeated the life stories of the youth active in their congregations, none of them talked about racism in light of their deeply held theological beliefs. None of the youth gave testimony about God's presence when affronted by racial profiling or racist insults, nor did they talk about God's power to transform racism. All of the teens understood racism as racial prejudice that they had encountered or observed. Although there was some sense of the institutional nature of racism, this was not explicitly expressed in their conversations. This chapter shares some of the Chicago teenagers' experiences of racial injustice, their understanding of racism, their expressions of despair concerning the perpetuity of racism, and the absence of language about God in relationship to racism.

First, I will introduce Mark, a member of a Baptist church, and Mary, a member of a Presbyterian church, who are both very active in their

congregations. I describe the theological motifs at the center of their spiritualities and lift up their thoughts about racism, followed by my analysis
of their meaning-making about racism in light of the theological motifs
in their life stories. Following Mark's and Mary's stories are those of a
cluster of teens from the Austin Community who talk about racism, in
response to a question about hope, using language popularized by media.
My analysis suggests that their hopelessness about racism is the result of
meaning-making through media ventriloquation — that is, speaking the
words of media or speaking the words of others that media construct,
so that youth are speaking through the voice of media. I conclude the
chapter with a constructive proposal consisting of emancipatory hope,
offering racism education as a means for the development of *oppositional
imagination* with black youth.

A Young Preacher's Spiritual Profile

Mark is fifteen years old, a ninth-grader from the Austin Community
on the west side of Chicago. Although once a vital community, Austin
is an economically distressed neighborhood.[1] During the Great Depression thousands of European immigrants moved further west in search of
work. Their vacated housing units were purchased by African Americans
from the South seeking employment in Chicago. In 1968, the assassination of Dr. Martin Luther King Jr. and the riots that followed left the
Austin Community, and homes and businesses in other parts of the west
side of Chicago, in ruins. This eventually led to disinvestment of businesses, unemployment, deteriorating property, and poverty persisting
through the 1990s.[2] There are territorial boundaries for rival gangs in
the Austin Community, much like those that separate other ethnically
dense neighborhoods in Chicago.

Mark believes that a personal spirituality is essential for his happiness, and he also takes responsibility for nurturing the spirituality of
other individuals in his church. Mark accepted his call to ordained ministry during the summer of 1994 in the Baptist church where his mother
and godparents also are members. Mark has "grown up in the church,"
and he cannot remember a period of time when he and his mother were
not attending every Sunday and several times during the week. However,
he also admits that although he has always attended church regularly,
he was not "converted" until the age of thirteen. He describes himself

as "a terror" prior to his conversion, noting, "I told people where to get off, I told them when to get on. And if you crossed me, I would let you know, you don't do that to me, . . . you don't run over [Mark] like that." A self-evaluation of his high-strung manner and juvenile high blood pressure forced him to rethink his attitude about people and life, in general. He said,

> I started to listen to people, and I started to see how, when I was acting like that, people would start to shy away from you. . . . When you [are] used to being around people, and they start to move away because you act [pauses] you start to check in the mirror and say, "Wait a minute, wait a minute, what am I doing?" . . . I got on another track, made a change in my life. When I made a change in my life, not only that, but as I came closer to people and most of all I came closer to God. That's really what changed me.

Mark's confessional statement reveals a theme of transformation much like many of the youth interviewed. Mark is most reflective about his past experiences of God's active presence in his life and how he views himself since his transformation. On November 20, 1994, he preached his "trial" sermon. He recalled, "I talked it over with my pastor and afterwards got up and confessed it in front of the church. . . . What a great pleasure and blessing I have that [I'm] able to expound on the word of God. God is giving you that gift to go out and preach to all nations." Although Mark is very confident in his calling as a young minister and preacher, he still talks about the realities and difficulties of growing up as a teenager. "The peer pressure that you have" is what he calls it.

It is not surprising that the most exciting religious moment in Mark's life was preaching his first sermon. When asked about this experience, this is what he said:

> I was eager to preach. I was not nervous. . . . I was ready for it, I was prayed up. I was ready to go and everything. . . . When I preached that first sermon, the feeling that knowing that it's the anointing of the Holy Ghost coming and speaking through me and giving me words to say [pauses] . . . to know that I am growing in God. I don't have to worry about what to say, because the Holy Spirit will speak through me and God will speak through me, that I can speak to his people. I think that to me, that was the greatest moment.

Mark displays confidence that "the anointing of the Holy Ghost" gives him words to say when he preaches to and teaches his congregation. Mark speaks with confidence regarding confronting peer pressure and violence in his school and community. He believes,

> Knowing that you know God...you don't have to be scared of things, knowing that when you reach a peak in your life where you feel like you cannot make it. It's good that you know God,...that you can make it, because you can read God's words you can find out, you can make it, that God can do anything but fail.

Mark emphasized the significance of the "Holy Ghost" in his life to fortify his confidence. He also understands the Holy Spirit as that entity of the Godhead who is "the comforter, the Spirit of teaching...a shield around me when I'm going to school, no matter how dangerous it is." Mark said he learned these theological dictums from his "pastor and various church members."

Mark exudes confidence in the power of the Holy Ghost to protect him from danger and anoint him with the right words when peers challenge him, but he fails to express his beliefs, particularly the power of the Holy Ghost, when he talks about racism. With a drop of rage in his voice, his response to a question about his hopes was, "That we stop all this racism, live together happily. Stop all this violence and shooting and killing one another...be together and be merry." When I asked Mark to define racism, he leaned forward and, with a black preacher's tempo, said,

> Racism. I define racism as just because I'm, I have this color, so you don't like me. Or just because I'm black, you think I'm not able...I'm not capable, or just because I'm a little poor or something, you think I can't do it, or I'm different. Or you think that you're higher up than me, when you came from the same race that I came.

He concludes his statement by saying, "Racism is everywhere. Racism to me is not only in whites...but there's a little racism...among blacks." Themes of God's infallibility, power to transform, convert, and protect, weave Mark's life story together. However, throughout his discussion of racism he fails to invoke his religious language about God and Holy Ghost as he did earlier in natural, animated conversation. Words such as "God can do anything but fail" and other religious language that expressed his hope in God are absent during the discussion on racism. Mark does not expect racism to stop, and he offers no commentary regarding God's activity in stopping racism.

An Honor Student's Spiritual Profile

Mary is a seventeen-year-old high school senior and honor student in Evanston, Illinois. This township of eight and a half square miles stretches north from the edge of Chicago and west from Lake Michigan. Evanston is a "college town," the location of Northwestern University and several other liberal arts and junior colleges, as well as a variety of professional and graduate schools. The population is predominantly white, at 71 percent, and between the ages of twenty and sixty-four.[3] The African American population is 23 percent, Asian and Pacific Islanders 4.8 percent, and other people of color 1.2 percent. Howard Street, on the south side of the city, is the borderline between Chicago and Evanston. Within a three-mile radius of Howard Street there is evidence of violent youth gangs and poverty.

As with Mark, transformation/conversion is also a dominant theological theme in Mary's life story. She uses the language of "commitment" and "call" as she reveals aspects of her spirituality. While describing her family, she emphasizes her African and white heritage. Her father is a Jamaican-born American, and her mother is a European American; both teach in public schools. Mary has many fond memories of growing up as the youngest of three girls. She and her older sister enjoyed participating in sports. The middle sister loved reading. When she and her sisters were very young, the family would visit her maternal grandparents in Ohio for Thanksgiving and Christmas. As they grew older, these holidays were celebrated at home. The memory of the ritual of dancing around the Christmas tree brings a smile to Mary's face.

Mary shared her experience of losing her fraternal grandmother, whom she had seen only twice. Mary knew her grandmother from the stories her father had shared. "This was a fantastic lady," said Mary. "I was really upset because I knew my dad was upset . . . he's never shown he is sad. . . . My grandma was part of a church he had left. And so he couldn't go to the funeral, he couldn't see her there. . . . I could tell he had been like crying . . . he was really upset." Mary went on to say that the reasons her grandmother's church would not allow her father to see his mother were cultic traditions and his defection from the church years earlier. "I was just so angry. . . . All he wanted to do [was] see his mom," said Mary.

This experience with the Jamaican church stands in stark contrast to that which Mary has experienced in her Presbyterian church. Church camp stands out as the pivotal moment when she committed herself to God. Years earlier she had attended church camp and "heard about Christianity," but she had not made a decision of commitment. The summer between elementary and junior high school was different for many reasons, including the absence of her sisters, fear of the imminent transition into junior high school, and three months of thoughtful preparation for the anticipated call to commit to God. The time was ripe for the commitment that Mary knew would change her life. She describes the event when the call to Christian discipleship was given:

> He [the leader] said, "Think about your life and everything." . . .
> They gave like . . . forty-five minutes. . . . And I just started crying, I
> don't know why. I just started crying, and I was, like, what I do will
> be for God. . . . I was just thinking about all I had and how God has
> given me my family, even the opportunity to be at this camp and
> everything, the opportunity to do well in school and everything,
> and how lucky I was. And I was *so* grateful.

Mary said that she was committed to God in speech and in actions. Although she is not as strict as she was initially, she is "still committed to God, but not in the same way." She now feels committed to God, but she is less rigid in her religious practices and in her isolation from other people. She says, "I realized God was, and still do now, that God was really there for me unconditionally. . . . That always makes me feel so good. . . . That God is still there regardless of if I'm doing the right thing or not."

Mary said that she learned of God's unconditional presence at church and at home, but particularly at church. Mary's words of God's unconditional presence are missing from her reflections on hope for humankind:

> Now this is our hope [but] I really don't know if they will **ever**
> become true: for peace in general, not just among nations or just

among everyone, understanding of each other's culture.... People say the United States is a melting pot, and then [*pauses*] you know, that's what they used to say. Then ... someone says it's not a melting pot, it's a salad bowl, because there are different pieces of everyone. In a melting pot, you're asking people to change, to melt into one. And we're not all one, and it shouldn't be all one, and everyone has different culture, and you shouldn't make someone lose their culture, you shouldn't melt everyone's culture into one. And I agree with that. So I hope everyone can understand each other's culture, and not have everyone be one culture, but understand each one's cultures.... I hope racism is gone. You know that's a given. I don't want racism, I don't want war.... I want everyone to have the same opportunity. I'd love a utopian system where everything is fine, everyone gets treated the same, everyone has opportunity to whatever, and there's no poor, everyone has healthcare, everyone is fine and no one is suffering.... It will not happen. I know not definitely in my lifetime.

Not only are Mary's beliefs about God's unconditional presence absent from the lengthy reflection on her hopes, but also she begins and ends with words of despair and doubt. Racism is the centerpiece of her litany of things she wants to end, bracketed by a concern for acceptance of cultures in their original state. Mary not only fails to refer to God's activity in ending racism and bringing peace, acceptance of diversity, and the end of suffering, but also defers to a utopian system rather than her belief in God. Mary contradicts earlier statements she had made regarding her intolerance of racism and any kind of unfairness to other people. Mary does not expect to be an agent of change in dismantling racism, nor does she expect racism to end, at least not during her lifetime. Both Mary and Mark articulate clearly their beliefs in God in most instances, except issues of racism and injustice.

A Fragmented Spirituality

Ministry intended to bring about emancipatory hope fosters an integrated spirituality that weaves together both pious and political ideological meanings. Religious belief and social practice are interrelated; they are intertwined. This way of being in the world manifests itself in a variety of forms, including language. Conversely, a fragmented Christian spirituality prohibits the weaving of language, belief, and practice.

Mark and Mary articulate a well-defined Christian spirituality shaped by concrete theological beliefs. Mark believes in transformation, God's protective presence, and God's infallibility. Reflecting on his conversion experience, he said, "When I made a change in my life, . . . I came closer to people and most of all closer to God. That's really what changed me." He is familiar with salvation language when describing his religious experiences. He said, "I was converted at a young age. . . . I confessed the Lord. I remember now that I told the preacher I wanted to get on that train, I wanted to get my ticket punched." Mark describes the "Holy Ghost" as the "Comforter" who helps him and places a shield of protection around him. A closer examination of Mark's thoughts about the Holy Ghost suggests that he has paraphrased and internalized portions of John 14, perhaps as taught to him in Bible study by his pastor and church school teachers: "But the Advocate, the Holy Spirit, whom the Father will send in my name, will teach you everything, and remind you of all that I have said to you. . . . Do not let your hearts be troubled, and do not let them be afraid" (John 14:26–27). More passionately he discusses "knowing God," which means he can persevere and survive when faced with obstacles and disappointments. He said, "Knowing that you can make it. I find that that's really what [religion] means to me. Knowing that you can make it, that God can do anything but fail. . . . Knowing that you have a savior that you can go to. You don't have to worry. . . . Just whatever the problem is, you can work it out." Knowing God and believing that God is infallible move Mark beyond moments of despair.

Mark demonstrates hope in God on a personal level, but he fails to invoke this type of language when discussing racism in society. Mark's hope ruptures in the face of racism. "My hope [is] . . . that we stop all this racism." His commentary on racism is cast in a language and tone of powerless anger for both Mark and the black community in general.

Mary, like Mark, used salvation language when she discussed her commitment to God and the transformative nature of that commitment. Opportunity to reflect on her blessings from God and to acknowledge thankfulness catalyzed her commitment to God. Initially, Christian commitment led her to practice a rigid and legalistic lifestyle. Eventually she grew to "realize that God was . . . really there" for her "unconditionally." Two essential components stand at the heart of Mary's religious beliefs:

(1) a changed life resulting from commitment to God; and (2) commitment to God because of God's unconditional presence and acceptance. Although these beliefs hold together in domains of family and church life, they fracture when Mary discusses racism. Where is God's unconditional presence in the midst of racism? Discussing her utopian desires, she states, "I hope racism is gone. . . . I don't want racism. . . . I want everyone to have the same opportunity. I'd love a utopian system where everything is fine . . . and no one is suffering. . . . It will not happen. I know not definitely in my lifetime." Mary juxtaposes these wishful thoughts of a "utopian system" with words of pessimism and despair. More interestingly, she captures the meaning of her thoughts in the language of a "utopian system" rather than language consistent with her theological beliefs of God's transformative power and unconditional presence.

Racism is racial prejudice and discrimination for Mark and Mary. Racism also is disjointed from their Christian beliefs in God who has the power to transform, convert, save, and protect. These youth failed to reveal how God acts regarding racism. In addition, their fragmented spirituality is historically inconsistent with the spirituality of African Americans of years past, especially as demonstrated in the life of Fannie Lou Hamer (as discussed in chapter 1). A fragmented spirituality such as that of Mark and Mary is incompatible with emancipatory hope — that intricately woven life of divine and human self-understanding that *expects* God's tranformative power and *acts in* God's transformative power against economic, political, and social domination. The theological themes of God who has power to transform, convert, save, and protect are the rudimentary ingredients of expectancy and agency, but Mark and Mary do not use them in this way. Although these beliefs are important to one's spirituality, without integration into and practice in the day-to-day confrontation with racism, they are merely seeds of emancipatory hope.

A Communal Appeal about Racism

EVELYN: What are your hopes for humankind?

DARYL: I never thought about it. . . . You know, doing the right thing, so we can all at least get along with one another regardless of what color we are.

Kathy, Betty, and Paul echo Daryl's response to the preceding question as they discuss their hopes about racism and violence. The question "Can't we all just get along?" circumscribes their meaning-making about ending racism and violence. But this question is not coupled with resistance language or religious language indicative of God's activity in ending racism and violence. Daryl hopes that "we can all at least get along with one another regardless of what color we are." Daryl believes that a wholesome spirituality involves being "sanctified . . . doing the Lord's work." However, when discussing harmonious living among diverse races, he does not offer similar religious language. Kathy hopes that "everybody just get along and stop all the violence against one another." She continues speaking firmly against violence and capital punishment. Kathy believes strongly in God's ability to transform wayward people such as her grandfather and herself. She also believes in the power of love to resurrect a person from the depths of despair. Yet her spiritual beliefs are not referenced when she discusses wholesome relationships between people at odds with each other. Betty, like Kathy, hopes that "everybody could just get along with each other." Paul states the same idea that Betty and Kathy express. He hopes that "everyone will become one, just get along." These four youths express a common plea that is disjointed from their deeply felt theological beliefs. Clips from their life stories reveal the theological themes that lace their identities together.

Daryl, Kathy, Betty, and Paul live with their families in the Austin Community. All are high school seniors except Betty, who is a tenth-grader. All are members of Baptist congregations and express the importance of religion in their lives. Family is also very important for them. Eighteen-year-old Daryl grew up with two sisters, two cousins, and both his parents, who, he boasts, "are still married now." He has been very careful to keep away from gangs, staying close to his sisters and cousins. However, the effects of gang violence touched his life when a close friend was shot and killed by gang members. Daryl had not seen his friend since eighth-grade graduation. "It was . . . really touching 'cause we grew up together, and it was really hard to believe he was gone. And he wasn't a gangbanger. He's just like me —you know, went to school and did his own thing and stuff. But he was in this car with a bunch of people and . . . they mistaken him for the wrong person."

Music is especially important for Daryl. He had the opportunity to sing "Lord, Lift Us Up Where We Belong" at his eighth-grade graduation. More exhilarating than singing at graduation was Daryl's participation in the men's choir with his father during a men's day program. "We went to church rehearsals mostly every Tuesday," said Daryl. When the day came for the program, "I was really hyped-up to do it. When I started marching down the aisles, everything came down on me." Daryl talked about not being ashamed to express his feelings as people who had known him since childhood smiled and called his name. "You know, it really made me feel good," said Daryl.

Daryl and his father attend church together every Sunday. With words of adoration, Daryl talks about his father and reveres him as his role model, the breadwinner for a family of five on the salary of a security officer. Daryl says, "My father is an established person. . . . He put the family together and he does what he has to do. [Sometimes] he acts crazy and talks crazy. . . . But when it comes down to serious business, he knows exactly what he is doing and he knows exactly what he wants. That's why I like him and I plan to do the same thing when I get around his age." Words of adoration for his father are tempered with joyous banter.

The theological motif of joy permeates Daryl's life story. He believes in being "sanctified . . . doing the Lord's work . . . going to church . . . praising [God's] word and doing the right things to help other people." The "Spirit inside you" brings Daryl joy. Specifically, singing in school and church brings him a joy that he is not ashamed to express publicly in tears and smiles.

Unlike Daryl, Paul has never known his father. This reality brought him to a low point in his life when he was in the eighth grade. "I saw fathers here, fathers everywhere," said Paul. "Seems like whatever went on, something had to do with a father, and my father [was] out of town." At least, that's what Paul would tell his teachers and classmates. "I was upset . . . mad, frustrated, sad we did not do everything else that fathers and sons do 'cause he was not there." Although Paul was once angry because his father was not around, he still embraces his mother and two older brothers as very important in his life. Paul's grandfather is also important for his spiritual self-understanding.

Paul believes that God transforms people. His own act of recommitment to God was the most exciting religious experience for Paul. His grandfather was the catalyst for his decision. Although he first joined the church when he was eight years old, he "rejoined" when he was fifteen. His grandfather had talked with him the night before his recommitment.

Prior to that discussion he had a "reality check." Paul said, "I was sittin' down, thinking, Living around there . . . if I don't try to do something with my life, I'll end up homeless, dead, a drug addict. . . . So I'll try to do something to keep me away from the crowd. So I figured there's nothin' else for me to do, so I'm ready to get my head straight." Paul was nervous at first because he had not attended church for more than a year. However, his determination pushed him past the butterflies in his stomach and down the aisle of the church. "When it happened, . . . a lot of tears everywhere. Grandmother and grandfather, they came up and hugged me. A lot of people were glad to see me back in church," said Paul.

Three years have passed since Paul's recommitment. His gradual transformation involves "reading the Bible sometimes and trying to understand it . . . [going] to my grandfather if I have questions . . . and take it step by step," explained Paul.

In Kathy's life story the theological themes of transformation and resurrection are interlocked with her love for her family. "I have a big family," said Kathy, "so you know it's a lot of love in a huge family." She leans forward and the tempo of her voice picks up when she speaks of her family. She lives with her mother and brother in the Austin Community. Kathy's grandfather, grandmother, aunts, uncles, and cousins all are from Chicago. It's not clear how many are from the Austin Community. Nevertheless, they find their way to each other during holidays and joyous celebrations, as well as in times of pain and grief. "Every year seems like the family gettin' bigger and bigger 'cause you meetin' people you ain't never met in you life before." She continues, "It's like everything you do . . . your family [is going to] be there," because life "consist of a lot of hurt, a lot of pain, a lot of misery, 'cause it's a lot of things happenin' when you're young."

The theological motif of resurrection is woven throughout Kathy's life story. She believes that love resurrects a person from the death of despair. During the lowest point in Kathy's life, November 1994, the resurrecting power of love from her family brought her back from depression. She describes her tragedy:

> In the same month . . . I lost three people I loved very much, that consist of my godfather, my uncle, and my brother. I loved them more than anything in this world. . . . One died, like, on a Sunday, the other died on Tuesday, and the other died on Thursday. It was

just back to back to back. I don't even think I could deal with none of that stuff. But I had family who loved me, and they brought me back. 'Cause I was at the point at where I would stay in the house. I wouldn't come to school, didn't talk to nobody, when I went in my room, locked my door, put my music on, and cried my self to sleep. I didn't eat for almost two weeks. Then my family . . . came over there, and they talked to me 'cause they loved me so much. They didn't want me going through what I was going through. They didn't want me to go through it alone, . . . so we talked about it and stuff. They brought me back up to speed, where I'm at now, 'cause it's, like, once you have the ones that you love, they will bring you from the lowest point straight back up.

Somewhat related to Kathy's experience of familial love is her belief about Easter. Discussing her favorite religious holiday and tradition, Kathy stated, "The biggest holiday for me . . . would be when Jesus died and came back and rose on Easter Sunday. . . . It's a lot of holidays, . . . by me being a Christian, it would've been when Jesus rose up."

Transformation is the other theological motif weaving together the *kente* cloth of Kathy's life. She values conversion or change in one's life — total movement away from old, destructive habits to new, wholesome ways of life. Like her grandfather, who once was "mischievous," Kathy has changed from a student who "ditched school" and hung out with the "wrong crowd" to one who now gives positive leadership to other students. A discerning teacher pulled Kathy aside and put her in the Peer Leadership Club. The changed Kathy is now a member of student council, swim team, and majorettes. She participates in Austin Youth, a neighborhood bureau of youth speakers who give talks against drugs and crime to students in elementary and junior high schools. Many of her friends are juniors, sophomores, and first-year high school students who warmly call her "cousin, sister, or aintee." With confidence she identifies herself as their role model and mentor. Like her grandfather, whose conversion experience she mentioned frequently, she has found what she wants to do with her life and is now sticking to it. Five years after his conversion, her grandfather accepted his call to ordained ministry and eventually started a new congregation. When asked about the beliefs and values she adopted from her grandfather, Kathy replied, "That you can change." Her litany of religious practices includes wearing skirts instead of pants, avoiding profane language, going to church frequently, studying the Bible daily, and getting involved in church activities. She concluded her list of practices by saying, "I don't consider myself as real religious. The only time I wear skirts is when I'm going to church...or for choir rehearsal....I don't like wearing skirts." Kathy ended our conversation just as she began, discussing various memories of her family.

Betty, like Kathy, reveres her family. She proudly describes her family as strong because they have been through so many "hard times and stuff." Betty describes herself and her family as survivors of endless episodes of death. The loss of close friends, family members, and a boyfriend who died from asthma have contributed to her sadness. "We stay together. There is much love we feel for each other," says Betty. Betty has many cousins in her family. They all were cheering for her when she graduated from the eighth grade. Betty's aunt stepped in to raise her nine siblings when Betty's grandmother died.

Betty's aunt and mother have greatly influenced her life. Many of Betty's values are adopted from her aunt, such as caring for others and being strong. Her aunt served as a surrogate grandmother for Betty and her cousins, who influenced Betty to go to church. When she was twelve, Betty was baptized in the Baptist church where her aunt was a member of the congregation. Betty describes her baptism:

> I was scared at first,...but...I just went through with it and I was happy. I went home braggin'....I think it was great. Now I want my brother to be baptized. So I think everybody should be baptized.

Betty also shared a similar list of religious practices that she feels are important. She said that a religious person "is somebody that commits, that goes to church every Sunday...that believes in the Bible...shouldn't have sex until you're married...that goes by the Bible." Betty adopted these beliefs from her aunt and her eighth-grade teacher. Both of these significant people "read the Bible all the time and talked about the Bible," said Betty. She admires her aunt's frequent church attendance, and she too attended church frequently after her baptism. Being with her family in worship is an essential part of religious life for Betty. However, since her aunt's death, her persistence in attending Sunday worship is no longer the joy it once was. Family, particularly her aunt, stands at the center of Betty's efforts to make sense of life, shaping her beliefs about religious practices. Her spirituality is shaped by love among her family members and the activities of worship, Bible study, play, and survival. The theological motif of joy is demonstrated in her thoughts about baptism and family life.

Daryl, Paul, Kathy, and Betty share similar beliefs about family, conversion, and religious practices. They even express their hopes for humankind in similar language: "Can't we all just get along?" Disturbingly, these youth, like Mark and Mary, demonstrate a fragmented spirituality. Deeply held religious beliefs and issues of race and violence are bifurcated. Their religious language and its meanings are split from their concerns about race and violence

Ventriloquating Media Culture

Interviews with Daryl, Kathy, Betty, and Paul were interspersed with their asking or paraphrasing the question "Can't we all just get along?" Where did the youth get this response? To use Mikhail Bakhtin's question, "Who precisely is speaking, and under what concrete circumstances?"

When I hear the words "Can't we all just get along?" it is as if I replayed the video clip of Rodney King speaking into the microphones of television reporters after rioting erupted in Los Angeles on April 29, 1992. Moments earlier a predominantly white jury in a suburban courtroom acquitted police officers who had been videotaped brutally beating motorist Rodney King. Media widely reported images and words of King's beating and the riots of south-central Los Angeles. At the peak of the riots, cameras showed Rodney King's face on television screens in the homes of millions of people, pleading for an end to the riots. King's words were immortalized by the media: "Can't we all just get along?" Daryl, Kathy, Betty, and Paul ventriloquate the Rodney King words, as these teenagers express little or no expectations regarding racial injustice and no beliefs of God's activity in ending racism.

The lacuna in data will not permit a firm conclusion concerning the compatibility of Rodney King's words to those of Daryl's, Kathy's, Betty's, and Paul's multivoiced community of parents, relatives, and friends. Nor can we determine the nature of the multivoiced community where Rodney King uttered the phrase "Can't we all just get along?" We can assume that within his community, whether family or church, those words, or some combination thereof, held meaning. Rodney King's words embody neither despair nor hope, but are a desperate plea in the midst of chaos.

The response of these teenagers begs three questions: Could African American youth relate so strongly to the experience of Rodney King that he was included in their multivoiced community? How influential were his image and voice for black youth? More importantly, what role did media play in the construction of Rodney King's voice and image, thus shaping the multivoiced community of black youth?

The words of Daryl, Betty, Kathy, and Paul suggest that they are a ventriloquation of media culture's construction of Rodney King. The words "Can't we all just get along?" were adopted, internalized, and voiced by these teens. Bakhtin defines the term "ventriloquation," according to James Wertsch, as "the process whereby one voice speaks through another voice type in social language: The word in language is half someone else's . . . it exists in other people's mouths, in other people's concrete contexts, serving other people's intentions: it is from there that one must take the word and make it one's own."[4] "Like the ventriloquist's dummy who speaks only the words of the ventriloquist, we speak only the words of others. But unlike the dummy, we struggle to appropriate these words and make them our own."[5] Words, before they are appropriated within us, are communal. They derive from one or more communities, one or more contexts, each defined by historical, cultural, and social particularities.

The process of appropriation is far from simplistic, but rather complicated, where words are strangers in our mouths for periods of time until the meanings we fashion from them feel at home in our larger schemes of meaning-making. This developmental process is what Bakhtin calls "ideological becoming." "The *ideological becoming* of a human being is the process of selectively assimilating the words of others."[6] Personal discourse is slowly shaped from the different speaking voices of one's "context and the various relationships and social interactions."[7] The multivoiced community may include mothers, fathers, grandparents, teachers, friends, employers, pastors, and even television personalities. They all offer competing points of view for the person ventriloquating, more often than not.[8]

Rodney King symbolizes the brutalization and dehumanization that black youths often experience at the hands of police and the legal system in the United States, particularly black males.[9] Poor and working-class African American youth harbor the "perception of being stalked and harassed and singled out," so much so that they "view the police department as just another gang that wears colors."[10] Jewelle Taylor Gibbs writes:

George Holliday, the amateur videographer, had managed to capture for the first time on film an unprovoked assault on a defenseless black man — a virtual lynching in full view of a public crowd, an unprecedented record of violence and victimization in late-twentieth-century America. The police had been accused of unprovoked and unjustified assaults against black males since Africans first set foot on American soil in 1619, but an actual beating had never been documented on film. The charges of police brutality against blacks had nearly always been denied by the police, disbelieved by the public, and dismissed by the courts.[11]

As the resulting events of Rodney King's beating unfolded — the trial and acquittal of the white police officers and the ensuing riots in south-central Los Angeles — African Americans across the country saw south-central Los Angeles as a symbol of all African Americans struggling in a racist society. During the peak of those riots, Rodney King's words sought to squelch the rebellion and rage. Television cameras showed the face and broadcast the voice of this "gentle giant"[12] pleading with rioters to stop the violence and looting as he posed the question "Can't we all just get along?" Rodney King's plea did not end the upheaval in south-central Los Angeles. However, through the help of mass media, he gave us an eternal phrase that is quoted over and over again as people despairingly search for resolution to conflict.

For many black youth, broadcast media, both radio and television, created a Rodney King image to which they could relate. As with adults, radio and television also created a Rodney King whose words they could adopt. Print and broadcast media created images of Rodney King the victim, the peacemaker, and, finally, the wife-beating brute. The media "contributed to much of the trashing of King's image and the erosion of any empathy for him as a tragic victim."[13]

Mass media — television, radio, magazines, tapes and CDs, videos, the Internet — play an important role in the lives of adolescents, and surveys indicate consistently high levels of media use among them.[14] Television viewing ranges from two to four hours per day, with some adolescents viewing up to eight hours per day. Differences in television viewing vary, depending on age, gender, ethnicity, and socioeconomic status. For example, during middle adolescence, television viewing usually decreases while radio listening and cinema attendance increase.

African American adolescents view television and listen to music more than European American adolescents do, with African American females showing the highest rate of viewing and listening.[15] Television and other media function as sources of information, coping, entertainment, sensation, gender role modeling, and youth culture identification.[16] Adolescents use television along with listening to music for coping with anxiety and unhappiness. Teens also obtain information that shapes their ideology from television and other mass media, especially beliefs and values about those topics that parents are reluctant to discuss. The Black Entertainment Network (BET) and MTV are two popular television networks that target African American adolescents with their programming. Their music videos and movie programs are particularly popular. MTV, however, primarily promotes the values and beliefs of its founders, three white males, whose political and moral beliefs dominate MTV programming. For example, MTV intermittently splices selective news briefs throughout music video programming and advertisements, shaping the language and beliefs of many young African American viewers. News briefs of racial injustice, particularly institutional racism, are rarely criticized by MTV's news reporters. When African American adolescents appropriate the words of MTV about racism into the intricate spaces of their psyche without critique, these youth are inadvertently ventriloquating media culture.

Ventriloquation of media culture regarding racism fragments the spirituality of adolescents who are in the throes of ideological becoming. The assimilation of words from characters and personalities on television who present a defeatist attitude for confronting racism prohibits youth from weaving together language, religious meaning, and moral practice that are indicative of expectation and agency for dismantling racism. Religious ideological becoming in youth requires appropriating the language and meanings of faith from significant individuals who are the depository of religious authority. These relations provide a religious authoritative voice. In any examination of media culture's power to fragment black adolescents' spirituality, consideration of the authoritative voice and the degree of responsiveness are important. Bakhtin suggests that authoritative voice and its internal persuasiveness shape the contours of ideological consciousness in adolescents.[17] Within the polyphonic environs of black adolescents lie religious culture, media culture, school culture, and family, all struggling for power to shape the consciousness of the adolescent. Although the values of these author-itative voices might intersect, they still compete for dominance in the meaning-making of youth. Media culture has the most dominant author-itative voice when black youth are persuaded to internalize political, moral, and religious beliefs that maintain white supremacy. When televi-sion is the authoritative voice drowning out all other voices of authority, black youth are socialized to maintain racism systematically, argues bell hooks.[18] Television, she maintains, socializes black youth to believe that their subordination is " 'natural' because most black characters are por-trayed as always a little less ethical and moral than whites, not given to rational and reasonable action."[19] When the psyches of black youth are bombarded daily by media culture that promotes white people as the ideal ontological model intellectually and physically, then internalized racist thinking is inevitable.[20] Internalized racist thinking is evident when black youth believe that being a good student or meditative while wor-shiping is "acting white." Such internalization about being in the world results from the ventriloquation of media culture and contributes to the dysfunctional ideological becoming of black adolescents.

Religious Meaning-Making as Oppositional Imagination

This chapter has focused on religious language and meaning-making about racism as an aspect of spirituality in African American ado-lescents. The foregoing descriptions and analyses argue that religious language and meaning that are compartmentalized indicates a frag-mented spirituality. That is to say, for youth to speak about God's salvific and protective power in their lives separately from the evils of racism experienced individually or collectively is a fragmented spirituality. The ideal spirituality for African American adolescents is a holistic or inte-grated spirituality that understands God's salvation even in the midst of racism. Central to this notion of a holistic or integrated spirituality are the religious language and the religious meanings that youth construct about racism and its eradication. What is the nature of such construc-tion in the lives of black teenagers active in their communities of faith? The church is challenged to consider what is involved in cultivating reli-gious language and religious meanings about racism that are indicative of a well-integrated spirituality in black youth. Fundamental to this challenge is consideration of the socialization of youth whereby language and meaning compliment the cause of dismantling racism. Churches must socialize youth in a way of thinking that informs meaning-making and in religious language that speaks about God's active presence in their lives and God's activity in ending racism. I suggest that the church socialize youth into *oppositional imagination* as a way of knowing.

Oppositional imagination means to resist one's present unseemly circumstance by envisioning alternatives to the situation. Oppositional imagination is an alternative way of thinking, an alternative worldview, that opposes racial domination. Elisabeth Schüssler Fiorenza uses the term "oppositional imagination" to describe the alternative world envisioned by people victimized by the domination of the Roman Empire in the first century. Followers of Jesus envisioned a world free of hunger, poverty, exclusive table community, bondage, sickness, and all forms of domination.[21] This oppositional imagination was captured in the idea of "*basileia* (commonweal/empire) of G*d as the alternative to that of Rome," writes Fiorenza.[22] Oppositional imagination means to resist economic, political, and cultural domination, which racism perpetuates, by visualizing a society free of racism. In short, oppositional imagination offers an alternative way of knowing.

Central to the Christian church's task of socializing black youth into oppositional imagination is the vocabulary that is passed on to youth. Charles Foster suggests that handing on the vocabulary of the Christian community is one of several educational tasks in building community. As such, members of the faith community experience the shaping of their perceptions as well as their identity.[23] However, when the vocabulary of the faith community stifles conceptual creativity for participating in God's transformation of injustice, the faith community must reconsider its vocabulary.

The church must help youth redefine terms that are central to their theological beliefs. Consider redefinition in light of the theological motifs woven throughout the life stories of the Chicago teens: transformation/conversion, recommitment, salvation, and resurrection. One of these theological motifs is a natural starting point for discussion about redefinition in light of oppositional imagination because it provides entry into the ideological concerns of a specific group of youth. Specifically, what if the Christian church helped African American adolescents think anew about racial domination in light of salvation? For some of the adolescents who told their life stories, salvation means personal confession and repentance followed by change of lifestyle. To be saved means your "sins" of dancing, partying, and hanging out with friends are forgiven. Lisa said, "The Bible says you have to confess with your heart and believe that penance should be done. To me, I think it means drastic change, meaning that once you are saved, you can't hang out with your friends the way you used to —you know, going to parties and things like that. . . . I could no longer participate once I become saved." In melancholic tones Lisa continued with a list of dos and don'ts to which she must adhere when she becomes saved. In addition to adhering to a strict legal code for saved youth, Lisa believes that salvation is personal holiness, between the individual and God.

Lisa and several other Chicago youth understand salvation as a private affair, referring to redemption from an unholy lifestyle and the guilt that it brings.[24] However, a redefinition of salvation from a social perspective encourages the possibility of formulating religious meanings that are connected to the political, social, and economic domains of our lives. "Salvation is social because sin is social," asserts James Evans.[25] He points out that sin is social because the sin of an individual not only offends God, but also injures other people.[26] Delores Williams also posits that salvation is social when we consider the context of "black Christians who want to be saved *in the material world.*"[27] She challenges African Americans with the urgency to strategize to "save their lives, churches, homes and communities" from oppressive social, political, economic, and legal systems.[28] For white oppressors, James Cone argues, salvation has "acquired a 'spiritual' connotation that is often identified with divine juice, squirted into the souls of believers, thereby making them better Christians and citizens."[29] Cone insists that salvation from the oppressor's point of view means maintaining the economic, political, and social status quo regardless of how it may hinder human flourishing.[30]

These womanist and black male liberation theologians help us understand salvation as a social, instead of private, affair. This redefinition of salvation provides the foundation for the reconfiguration of the theological motif of salvation within the epistemology of African American adolescents. As such, black adolescents can reimagine personal salvation in relationship to the social ills of society, including racial domination.

Additionally, a broader understanding of salvation, as discussed here, coupled with broader meanings for sin is essential to the redefinition process. Missing from the rhetoric of the Chicago teenagers is an understanding of racism as sin, a human evil that injures both God and racially oppressed people whom God created. Sin understood as violation of a moral "spiritual" code is shallow and naive. Sin is an infraction of our covenant with God, ourselves, and others. Sin is a disruption of our relationship with God and humankind.[31] Racism, for me, is by far the most demonic manifestation of sin that diabolically severs covenantal relationships. Basically, I am suggesting an enhanced sociological and theological vocabulary for which the Christian community must be held accountable for developing in African American adolescents so that oppositional imagination will become a way of knowing for them.

Notes

1. Stacey Flint, "Empowerment Zones: Are the Critics Right? A Case Study of Chicago's West Side Empowerment Zone," *http://flintspark.com/uplan/empzones.htm.*

2. Ibid. Also, the Chicago Public Library Austin Branch Community Profile gives the following: 1990 census data indicates that the Austin Community is 94.8 percent African American, 3.5 percent white, 1.4 percent Hispanic, .2 percent Asian American, .1 percent Native American.

3. Electronic database, *www.cityofevanston.org,* "Facts and Figures," 1.

4. James V. Wertsch, *Voices of the Mind: A Sociocultural Approach to Mediated Action* (Cambridge, Mass.: Harvard University Press, 1991), 59.

5. Lyn Mikel Brown, *Raising Their Voices: The Politics of Girls' Anger* (Cambridge, Mass.: Harvard University Press 1998), 105.

6. M. M. Bakhtin, *The Dialogic Imagination,* ed. Michael Holquist (Austin: University of Texas Press, 1981), 341.

7. Brown, *Raising Their Voices,* 106.

8. Ibid.

9. See Jewelle Taylor Gibbs, *Race and Justice: Rodney King and O. J. Simpson in a House Divided* (San Francisco: Jossey-Bass, 1996).

10. Ibid., 73.

11. Ibid., 30.

12. Ibid.

13. Ibid., 111.

14. See G. A. Fine, J. T. Mortimer, and D. F. Roberts, "Leisure, Work, and the Mass Media," in *At the Threshold: The Developing Adolescent,* ed. S. S. Geldman and G. R. Elliott (Cambridge, Mass.: Harvard University Press, 1990), 245.

15. See John W. Santrock, *Adolescence: An Introduction,* 6th ed. (Madison, Wis.: Brown & Benchmark, 1996).

16. Ibid.

17. Bakhtin, *The Dialogic Imagination*, 342–43.

18. See bell hooks [Gloria Watkins], *Killing Rage: Ending Racism* (New York: Henry Holt, 1995).

19. Ibid., 114.

20. Ibid., 117.

21. Elisabeth Schüssler Fiorenza, "To Follow the Vision," in *Liberating Eschatology: Essays in Honor of Letty Russell*, ed. Margaret A. Farley and Serene Jones (Louisville: Westminster John Knox Press, 1999), 135.

22. Ibid.

23. See Charles Foster, *Educating Congregations* (Nashville: Abingdon Press, 1994).

24. James H. Evans Jr., *We Shall All Be Changed: Social Problems and Theological Renewal* (Minneapolis: Fortress Press, 1997), 64.

25. Ibid.

26. Ibid.

27. Delores S. Williams, "Straight Talk, Plain Talk: Womanist Words about Salvation in a Social Context," in *Embracing the Spirit: Womanist Perspectives on Hope, Salvation and Transformation*, ed. Emilie M. Townes (Maryknoll, N.Y.: Orbis Books), 98.

28. Ibid., 104–5.

29. James Cone, "Black Theology and Black Liberation," in *Black Theology: A Documentary History*, rev. ed., vol. 1, ed. James Cone and Gayraud Wilmore (Maryknoll, N.Y.: Orbis Books, 1993), 110.

30. Ibid.

31. Daniel L. Migliore, *Faith Seeking Understanding: An Introduction to Christian Theology* (Grand Rapids: Eerdmans, 1991), 130.

CHAPTER THREE

"I'M MIXED"

The Politics of Racial Identity

"Junior high, that was a turning point, especially when I got to the eighth grade. Well, I had a *major* transition from then on, because I'm mixed," declared Mary. This seventeen-year-old honor student from Evanston Township High School had shared warm stories of Christmas with her parents and two older sisters and of her athletic and academic achievements. As she turned from childhood memories to those of junior high school, she shared emotional scenes of negotiating her racial identity. Mary's story captures the focus of this chapter: the politics of racial identity, development, and its effects on the spirituality of black adolescents. By "politics" I mean the negotiation of acceptable behavior, mores, and folkways with regard to one's racial self-understanding. Central questions are: What are the primary concerns of the Chicago teens as they fashion their racial identity? How do perceptions about skin color affect racial identity formation in black teens? How is skin color related to class? How do skin color and class impact black adolescent spirituality? Emancipatory hope responds to colorism, the internalized self-consciousness about skin color, as an aspect of black adolescent spirituality.

In this chapter I present the life stories of Mary, Ellen, and Kermit as they reflect on issues of colorism. I lift up and analyze salient issues of racial identity related to colorism. I offer a summary of identity development theory and racial development theory. I attempt to illustrate victory over shame through texts from the Bible. I briefly conclude with a challenge to the church in regard to enabling black youth to move beyond the shame of colorism to self-worth.

Torn between Black and White

Mary, the honor student whose spiritual profile was presented in chapter 2, has another aspect to her story. She struggled with fashioning an identity as a biologically mixed-race person. As we talked, she stressed the social events of her life and her negotiation of a biracial identity.

All up until maybe eighth grade, or fifth grade, I sit at the lunch table with everybody. It didn't matter. And then junior high, things started to splitting up. My best friend from elementary school was a white girl... because we were taking the same classes all the time. So especially in junior high, the classes started really splitting up where I was in advanced classes... there were, like, one maybe two blacks. I mean, I'd be, like, the only one if not one more person in there.... It didn't bother me because I didn't care at that time. But then lunchtime came, and I'd sit with my best friend. I guess I'd think now I was with all whites. And it didn't bother me until eighth grade, and it *really* started bothering me.... Everybody thought I was, you know [*pause*] they knew. I mean, they thought I was a good kid and everything, and... then I started hearing kids calling other kids names — I mean, like "Oreo" and other stuff. And I started thinking, well... I started not being comfortable because I started being with, I was still with all whites and I had black friends. I had a lot of black friends, but, like, my best friend used to be a white girl, so I was still hanging around with her. And I really got... uneasy. So... I changed on my own, I think.... I changed on my own, and it was really a big change. I started sitting at *the* table, I didn't go straight from the whites to the blacks.... The only mixed table that there was, they were my friends. I didn't change because I didn't — I mean, they were my friends, so I started going there. That was a major change for me, because... I know my other sisters had to go through this too, but it was my own initiation.

Mary is the youngest of three daughters. Her father is "black," she said. "He's from Jamaica. And my mom is white. She's from Chicago." Both parents are schoolteachers in the Chicago area. Mary identified herself as a mixed or biracial person but struggled with the dilemma of choosing friends from either or both the white and black racial groups. She also struggled with being the only one in white classes — something that didn't bother her prior to the eighth grade. The problem of being associated with whites climaxed during lunch period. The choice of a racial group with whom to socialize was understood as an "initiation" — something both her older sisters had experienced. She had considered seeking her sisters' advice because "they all had been there, but . . . this is something that I did. . . . I just, I went and changed, and eventually I got to like black kids and whatever. I just felt more comfortable, after awhile." Mary continued, "I could not relate, you know, [to] the white kids telling the story of home or whatever. I just didn't relate."

When Mary became a ninth-grader, she welcomed the new experience of being in high school, although with some anxiety and apprehension. She met her first boyfriend and new friends, and also reacquainted herself with old friends from junior high school. Mary recalls,

> So it was an exciting time. It was scary, but it was neat to go into some of the new stuff. . . . I was still in all-white classes. But I always hung out with my black friends, and that was a difference because I had no white friends. . . . My friends were all blacks. But I was really comfortable. So the problem was I was uncomfortable in class. . . . I did my work and got my A's and stuff, but I didn't say anything in class. And then outside of class, totally different. People who were in my class were so surprised when they found me with my friends and I was smiling, goofy and stuff like that. That was my freshman year.

At first, Mary spoke of her self-confidence in academics and her lack of confidence in extracurricular activities. But eventually she pushed herself to achieve prowess in basketball and track. As a senior, Mary felt "liberated" and unencumbered with peer dress codes. She was proud of her academic achievements:

> I'm, like, the only black person in . . . the top twenty kids in my class. And that might not be much, [*laughs*] but ah, it's good. I mean, I need to stay there. I feel pressured to stay there . . . from teachers, from everybody, because if I don't, then I feel that if it's all whites in there, then . . . it looks like only white people succeed, or that white people are smarter. I don't want people to say that blacks can't succeed. . . . And I know a lot of kids . . . friends I know . . . could have been easily up where I am . . . if they were given a chance. But I lucked out because of the tracking system when I was in elementary school . . . they put me in a higher class. My other friends are *very* capable.

Mary continued her critique of the tracking system in school, saying, "Others worked just as hard, but were not placed in honors classes."

In the context of her school and peers, Mary chooses the African American or black racial identity. Mary takes pride in her identity as a black student who is an achiever, defying stereotypes of black teenagers as being incapable of academic achievement.

In the context of the church, Mary reveals little if any evidence of the racial identity dilemma she faces at school of identifying herself as black, white, or mixed. Mary and her mother and sisters are active members of a predominantly white Presbyterian church. She says that her father rarely attends church with the family because "he was so affected by his church in Jamaica when he was young. . . . It really made him pessimistic about churches." She goes on to explain that her father is "not opposed to the Scriptures. He surprised me that he is very versed in the Scriptures." He did not approve of the people who attended their church. "He thought that they were corrupt . . . the clergy and stuff." She goes on to explain that her father found problems similar to those he had found in the church of his childhood in Jamaica existing in the family's present church in Evanston. Nevertheless, Mary's father never dissuaded the family from attending church.

Mary said that she learned her beliefs about God at church in Sunday school, the church youth group, and at home.

> We're not that religious at home, but that is one of the things that, you know, is always stressed. . . . We'd go to church and we'd . . . come back. . . . We don't, like, sit down and talk about church, but if there was something that was pointed out in our Sunday school and stuff, someone would say something, and we talked about it a little bit.

You will recall that the theological themes of conversion and God's unconditional presence are central to Mary's spiritual profile. She commented that her father believes, as she does, "that God was really who's there for me unconditionally." Mary continued,

> And that's the thing. . . . When something goes wrong, some friend does something bad to me . . . the one who's always there is God. . . . And even though I'm not as good or Christian, whatever, as I was, the one thing that always stuck with me is that, and that always makes me feel so good. I mean, I always recognize that God is still there regardless if I'm doing the right thing or not.

Additionally, Mary talked about God's will for her life, "to do the best I can in everything, to try my hardest." She continued,

> I don't have to succeed if my best does not make me succeed. But to do my best and then to help others...to lift them up. I'm not talking financially, I'm talking about just to help them in their life, not even to convert [them]....I mean, I'm not even out to convert anybody. I don't think that God says I have to convert people. I think that God says I need to help others and help myself, and that I need to do my best.

Mary's conversation about her experiences in Sunday school, youth group, and church camp do not indicate the dilemmas related to racial identity that she experienced at school.

I Know Who I Am

Themes in Mary's story intersect with those of Ellen's story. Both girls are biracial but identify themselves in the social realm as African American.

"When I was young," Ellen said, "it was me, my mom, my two brothers, and . . . , well, I'm biracial. My mother's white and my father's black." It was as if this fifteen-year-old sophomore anticipated the question that many racially mixed people are asked: "Where are you from?" For some puzzling reason, Ellen wanted to clarify her racial identity to me at the onset of our conversation. Perhaps my intense gaze, intending to communicate sincere listening, reminded her of the many questioning eyes that wondered about her light skin. Whatever her reason, Ellen's opening words about the "the beginning" of her life described her beloved family and its racial makeup, thus defining her racial identity.

Juxtaposed with her declaration of racial identity was the assertion that she once had attended Sunday worship, Wednesday Bible study, and choir rehearsal regularly with her paternal grandmother. Ellen said that she especially liked singing in the choir. However, since sixth grade, when her parents divorced and Ellen, her mother, and her brother moved to the north shore of Chicago, she seldom has attended church. She credits her father for the principal religious value that guides her life, a spiritual mantra drawn from Matthew 7:12, "In everything do to others as you would have them do to you," and Luke 6:31, "Do to others as you would have them do to you." She said, "Without sounding like, whatever, I truly,

truly, truly believe that you should do unto others as you would like others to do unto yourself. 'Cause that's . . . that was one of the things that my father always says to you — like, what goes around comes around."

Her belief is so strong and intense that she "fear[s] that something bad would happen" to her if she does not do unto others as she would have them do unto her. With warm memories of attending church with her paternal grandmother and of her father's golden rule, Ellen locates the site of her Christian spiritual formation.

Family is a high priority for Ellen. Family is "some sort of a center," said Ellen. She described the most significant people in her life this way:

> My mother, because she — she's real intelligent and she did a lot of things on her own. And, well, where she was raised, it was an all-white community. And I guess . . . she moved to California and, well, she met . . . my father, and, I don't know, she lost a lot of her connections to where she was living, and people didn't like her — people, you know, blah, blah, blah. But I guess that didn't matter. . . . She did a lot of things on her own, and she got a good education on her own, and she has a real good job now on her own, and, you know, she has a nice house, nice car, and, you know, she takes care of her children, and she does a lot of things on her own, and she's real self-sufficient. And my dad, he's just really intelligent, and he's an astrologer — well, he's more into spiritual things, how everything has a spirit, like trees and stuff, like, everything has a spirit. And he's always saying that people, like, the human race does so many bad things to the environment, and whatever goes around comes around. That's why the environment does so many bad things to the human race. . . . So he's really into the spiritual aspect of things, and he's just real intelligent, and he's a real strong man.

As our conversation progressed, she discussed the importance of education to every aspect of life. Ellen believes that most problems can be solved through personal initiative to become educated. "Because nobody looks down on an educated person," she said. When I asked Ellen to discuss oppression, she described it as those who have been put down or made to feel inferior. Ellen feels that oppression is a combination of people being devalued and their subsequent self-loathing mentality. "I will never devalue another African American person," she said. "I would never do that, just because it seems, just wrong I guess, you know. And I would never take the mentality of just thinking that I don't have any value, or just thinking I'm not going to do anything, go any- where anyway, so why try or think that I'm better playing basketball, so I'm not going to try to learn....Just the oppressive ideas — I don't even plant them in my mind. Especially at a young age, I don't want to do that."

She believes that education is the key to overcoming oppression and self-loathing. She maintains, "If you educate yourself, especially about who you are and where you've come from, then you will see that there's no reason for you to be oppressed." Ellen believes that there are "people who let themselves be oppressed."

Ellen enjoys reading African American literature almost as much as she enjoys her drama classes. She likes Maya Angelou and Angela Davis because "they see strength within the black woman, I guess....I don't know [if] they see strength. And they are positive....And you know Langston Hughes. He's, he's really good. And W. E. B. Du Bois. I think he's real good. I don't necessarily like Booker T. Washington. He seems sort of negative to me." Ellen's remarks about black intellectuals included a lengthy commentary on Richard Wright, and then compared Washington with Du Bois.

> And Richard Wright — I just got finished reading *Black Boy*. For some reason, I mean, after I read the book, ...I went to the library and I was finding these articles about him. And he went to Paris, and he married a white woman, and he had kids, and he, you know, he's always talking about the North and stuff like that. And it seemed to be that he was sort of, I don't know, not necessarily a sellout, but it seemed like he was afraid to grasp any kind of thing in the African American community. It seemed to me that he was so fearful of it that he couldn't accept himself as a black person....That was my analysis of...his life. Though it was good, but I didn't necessarily — I like people who are, who find strength within themselves, and who are, who look at, define themselves, and think who they are is beautiful. And that's what I like, and he didn't show that, and neither does Booker T. Washington.

As our conversation came to a close, Ellen indicated that her values of self-reliance and self-sufficiency come from both her parents. "Self- sufficiency is real important to him [her father]....Mom always wants me, she always tells me, to respect myself. Well, so does my father. I guess they share a lot of the same values. . . . And my mom is always saying that I'm beautiful. You know, who you are is really beautiful. She always says that, and she's, like, no matter who says what, you're still beautiful."

Both Ellen and Mary believe that education is an important value and struggle with the educational practice of tracking. On the other hand, these girls differ in their understanding of oppression. Mary blames white powers of authority for racial injustice; Ellen believes that oppression is a state of mind.

I'm Not Mixed!

Like Mary, Kermit struggles in choosing between black or white friends. However, Kermit is not biracial. His thoughts highlight his desire to dismantle stereotypes that imply that light-skinned people are biracial and live in the suburbs.

"My dad looks basically like Tom Selleck. If you didn't know, if you weren't from the South, you'd probably think he was white almost. My mom has weird hair. They're both really light-skinned." Since Kermit had told me that his parents were from Louisiana, I asked if they were Creoles. He didn't know. Then he responded, "I think way back in the family line somewhere there is a Native American. And I guess somehow the gene has gone all the way through the family, because everyone in this family has hair like this [*pointing to his straight hair*], and really light-skinned. People used to think I was mixed." Kermit continued, "It's been really a battle for me to convince them: No, both my parents are black." Kermit's dilemma is not choosing which racial group to associate with, but convincing other African Americans that he is not mixed. Kermit also discusses the related issues of class to the problem of racial identity.

And also socially my family, we live comfortably, we live in the suburbs. My dad is a captain for an airline. I don't have to struggle for anything. . . . My parents have a lot of black friends. But I grew up around ninety-nine percent white people. . . . In elementary school, you know, no one noticed. Kids are kids, you know, everyone is the same. When I started through middle school, it was just like — especially when I got to high school — it was just like this: *boom,* you got all the white kids on one side of the room and all the black kids on another side of the room. In a way I did feel for awhile, I had almost to convince myself that I wasn't mixed, because I had come up, I've been raised around white people, and all my friends basically had been white. And so you know, that's where I...felt comfortable....Then there was the other side in me that was saying, you know, "Where is your background? Where is your African American culture? You should be hanging around more with our kids." I don't think I really got any problem. By the time you get to high school, things like name calling, stuff you do in elementary and middle school — I went through that barrage of "Oreo" and things like that because of the way I talk and stuff like that. You get to high school, and people just mature, and that phased away. So there wasn't any real peer pressure: you should only be hanging around black kids....So the peer pressure wasn't there. But there was, like, struggle going in my mind: What should I do?

In addition to choosing black or white friends, Kermit introduced other issues related to race and class identity when he spoke of hair texture and living in the suburbs versus the inner city.

Beginning with his ninth-grade year, Kermit has been on three mission trips with the youth group of his church. He described these mission trips as the most exhilarating religious experience he has had. His first mission trip stands out more than any others:

In Washington, D.C., we worked with the homeless at a homeless shelter, and did a vacation Bible school in the afternoon for kids. I never really liked little kids that much, but it was just, like, seeing all these little kid coming, like, they were so happy. I'm sure that they weren't really understanding everything that we were teaching them, but it was something that I felt like I was giving something back. Whether or not it really had an impact, at least it was there. And then the camping trip in the Black Hills of North Carolina....It was so exhilarating to be out there in nature. The leaders we had on the camping portion were people who majorly appreciated the vastness, the beauty — this is God's creation, untouched by cities and factories and industries. How beautiful it is to be up there in the mountains.

Kermit went on to describe a twenty-four-hour silent retreat that he participated in during the weeklong camping trip.

> Basically, they gave us, like, a tarp and a jug of water and our sleeping bags. And we went out by ourselves...just off the trail, and it was, like, one hundred yards on either side of each person. You have nothing else to do, and they gave you a Bible. You don't have any distractions, then you start to hear all the little chipmunks and squirrels and everything running around. You get, like, totally engulfed in everything around you and start thinking really deeper. I never really had an experience where I think that Christ had appeared to me or someone had shown me the light. But I think that was just, like, a really deep experience—being out there away from the city and being absolutely alone for twenty-four hours. You know, it was trying. It rained, and we had to sleep under those little tarps...it actually was a poncho.... You tried to tie the hood up, and it just leaked all over you, and you're totally wet. Sitting at home...in a room for twenty-four hours, you think you'd go insane. But it was, like, well, I made it. It was really cool.

Continuing to reflect on his twenty-four hours of silence, prayer, and reading the Bible, Kermit said that he "read the whole book of Genesis, which I can't remember much of any more." He adds, "I always thought that it was really God out there, and he is omnipotent, omniscient, that prayer, speaking out loud is.... You define more about your life through your actions rather than what you pray for."

Conflicted about Racial Identity

As Mary, Ellen, and Kermit fashion a personal identity, their primary concern is in the domain of racial identity. In this section I will analyze the primary issues of the development of racial identity for these teens. "Racial identity development is defined as pride in one's racial and cultural identity."[1] Salient issues include declaring a racial identity, selecting a racial peer group, struggling with stereotypes about black teens, and struggling with color consciousness or colorism and its relationship to social class. These issues are related to developmental aspects of self-concept—that is, the personal ascription of positive and negative characteristics, the conglomerate of abilities, whether valued or devalued, that form a cohesive self-understanding.[2]

Some biracial teenagers, like Mary and Ellen, struggle with declaring a racial identity. A biracial person is a first-generation mixed-race person who is the product of an interracial relationship between people of two different racial groups.[3] An example is the offspring of an Asian American father and a European American mother. Mary and Ellen are children of a father from African descent and a European mother. Mary chooses an African American identity when in the context of her school. However, in church her choice of racial identity is unclear. One can imagine that Mary experiences the unconditional acceptance of the church regardless of her racial heritage; therefore, claiming a racial identity is not her concern. On the other hand, Mary may identify herself as biracial or function under the "color-blind" mode — that is, seeing beyond race and responding as a person without race, or "raceless," in her congregation. Racelessness is a strategy for acceptance for someone situated within a white majority. Some academically successful African American students have utilized this strategy in order to be accepted among their white peers. Those black students seeking to assimilate into the dominant group de-emphasize characteristics that might identify them as members of the minority group.[4] The congregation may also respond to Mary in a "color-blind" manner, acknowledging her identity in such a way that supersedes racial identity.

Ellen, however, clearly identifies herself as biracial. Within the context of her identity, she does not appear to vacillate between racial identities. Ellen is biracial at school, at home, and even while attending a predominantly black church with her African American grandmother. Ellen's identity as biracial in an African American congregation is not a difficult task. Historically, the black church accepted mulatto children born as a result of miscegenation or rape by white slaveholders.[5]

Mary is concerned about selecting a racial peer group, most pressingly during junior high school. Her dilemma in the school cafeteria revolved around her decision about which lunch table to choose: with her white friend, or with her black friends at the "black" table. The choice of a lunch table is the metaphorical choice of a peer group. During junior high school Mary makes the decision to leave behind her best friend from elementary school, a white girl, and choose black students as her immediate peer group.

Beverly Daniel Tatum, a teacher and researcher on issues of racial identity development in teenagers, describes this phenomenon in her book *"Why Are All the Black Kids Sitting Together in the Cafeteria?"* Tatum argues that regardless of whether or not school children stay together from kindergarten through eighth grade, children group themselves according to race by the sixth or seventh grade.[6] Significant to this developmental change is the onset of puberty, she argues, and I would add to that the capacity for abstract thinking. For black youth, this includes ethnic and racial identity. Mary's experience mirrors that of black youth that Tatum describes.

A Word on Identity Development

For Mary, Ellen, and Kermit, themes of race and class hover around their quest for identity. Negotiating the political terrain of racial identity is particularly important for them. Even though it is only one component of their total identity matrix, racial identity may influence sexual, spiritual, gender role, and other aspects of identity. A discussion of racial identity development theory can illuminate the central concerns of these three adolescents. However, before discussing racial identity development, I must mention some of the earlier cognitive and psychoanalytic theories that provide a wider rubric for a discussion of racial identity development. These theories offer general information on the developmental capacity for understanding the framework of adolescent thinking about racial identity.

A consideration of major theories of adolescent development moves the discussion into a broader context and reveals a lacuna of research and theory on the race-sensitive aspects of adolescent development.

Let us begin with theories on cognitive development, or conscious thought.

The Swiss developmental psychologist Jean Piaget argued that adolescents construct their own cognitive worldviews because of their capacity for abstract thinking. In Piaget's four-stage theory, the fourth and final stage, the formal operational stage, which he believed emerges from eleven to fifteen years of age, is the stage for abstract thinking. Adolescents no longer are limited to actual, concrete experiences that anchor their thoughts.[7] Formal operational thinking allows adolescents

to develop "purely hypothetical possibilities or strictly abstract proposi-
tions" and the capacity to reason logically about their thoughts.[8] During
early adolescence, formal operational thought consists of "unconstrained
thoughts with unlimited possibilities" as well as "excessive assimilation as
the world is perceived too subjectively and idealistically."[9] In late formal
operational thought, adolescents test out the results of their reasoning
against experience, and a consolidation takes place; an intellectual bal-
ance is reached. Idealism and thought filled with possibilities accompany
the abstract nature of formal operational thinking.[10] As such, adolescents have the capacity to think about ideal qualities and characteristics
in themselves and others. Such thoughts usually lead teens to compare
themselves to others in regard to ideal standards. Teens dream of a world
of peace and harmony, a perfect church, and a perfect family.[11] In early
adolescence, idealism may be accompanied by parental criticism, and
the young teen imagines ideal parents with whom his or her parents fail
in comparison.[12] By measuring parents against an ideal and acknowledging the imperfection of his or her parent, the teen can justify withdrawing
some love from the parent and giving it to friends or other adults during
the process of individuation.[13] For middle and late adolescence, idealism involves the coupling of altruism or unselfish concern to help others
with trust in the possibilities that such acts of kindness will yield a better
society.[14]

In addition to theories about formal operational thinking, there is a
contextual theory on cognitive socialization that stresses that "the cognitive growth of children and adolescents is aided by the guidance of
individuals who are skilled in the use of the culture's tools."[15] Central
to this toolkit is the use of language and worldview. Lev Vygotsky developed this theory during the late 1800s. Contemporary proponents of his
theory, such as Barbara Rogoff and Urie Bronfenbrenner, have focused
primarily on children. James Garbarino, a student of Bronfenbrenner,
has focused on the social environments of adolescent boys and their comprehensive effects on cognition. I mention these developmental aspects
of cognitive development, both formal operational thought and social
cognition, because they provide an understanding about the capacity of
adolescent thinking and identity.

Psychoanalytic theories focusing on unconscious thought provide an
equally important perspective. As an aspect of psychosocial development,
adolescents across racial and ethnic groups ponder their identity: Who

am I? Who is like me? How am I different? These questions are just a few of the many questions of identity that are prominent during the developmental period of adolescence and reflect on a portion of the total identity matrix.[16] Erik H. Erikson is considered by some scientists to be the single most influential psychologist on adolescent identity formation. He designated the fifth developmental stage in the human lifecycle, identity versus identity confusion, as that stage that individuals experience during adolescent years.[17] During this time, adolescents struggle with who they are as sexual, spiritual, political, and social human beings. This is a time when adolescents experience a necessary turning point, a crucial moment or crisis in identity.[18] Erikson also coined the term "psychosocial moratorium," which means a delay of adult commitments and also a period in which society selectively permits a kind "of provocative playfulness" of youth.[19] A moratorium leads youth toward deeper commitment after a transitory phase and confirmation of youth's commitment on the part of society.[20] While in the liminal stage between childhood and adulthood, adolescents experience a moratorium as part of their identity exploration.[21]

Values and beliefs are shaped as teenagers come to know who they are. Ontological questions about the essence of one's existence, as well as epistemological questions of what is true, are immediate concerns for teenagers in late adolescence, eighteen years of age up to their midtwenties.[22] However, I posit that life's circumstances, such as the existential realities of poverty and death, may force a sixteen-year-old into questions about his or her personal existence. The ability not only to think about such existential questions but also to reflect and step away to "engage in analyses of prior analyses" is the capacity for formal operational thought.[23] This form of thinking about thinking, cognition beyond the concrete to the abstract, allows the adolescent to contemplate issues related to personal ideology. Ideology, "a systematic scheme or coordinated body of ideas and beliefs concerning human life and culture," is an important aspect of identity during adolescence.[24] The search for identity sets youth apart from children as the central, virtually universal, concern during adolescence. Erikson, in *Identity, Youth, and Crisis*, has widely influenced the understanding of identity formation during adolescence for researchers in the social sciences. Erikson argues that during stage five of the human development lifecycle, "identity versus identity confusion," youth experiment with many roles of the culture. During this crisis of discovering who one is and what one is about, adolescents strive to resolve the crisis of discovering who they are. Or, on the other hand, as a result of role confusion, the teen totally loses himself or herself to peers or withdraws socially.[25] Identity formation is a process that involves commitment to an ideological stance, a sexual orientation, and a vocational direction.[26]

James Marcia, an Eriksonian researcher, has developed Erikson's theory into four strata of identity so that empirical study of Erikson's theory would be facilitated.[27] Adolescents classified by these modes are defined in terms of "the presence or absence of a decision-making period (crisis) and the extent of personal investment (commitment) in the areas of occupation and ideology."[28] These four modes of resolving identity crisis, predominantly in late adolescence, involve (1) identity diffusion, (2) identity foreclosure, (3) identity moratorium, and (4) identity achievement. In this model, one considers the extent of the teen's crisis and commitment in order to classify the adolescent according to one of the four statuses.[29] Crisis means a period of identity development when the adolescent chooses among meaningful alternatives.[30] This is a decision-making period.[31]

Put another way, the adolescent is exploring life choices of values, beliefs, attitudes, and careers. Commitment implies an aspect of identity development wherein the "adolescent shows a personal investment in what they are going to do."[32] Adolescents show some degree of personal investment ideologically and occupationally.[33] Since racial identity involves ideology, I will classify identity status in terms of ideological direction. (1) Identity diffusions occur when young people have no set ideological direction, regardless of whether or not they have experienced a decision-making period or crisis. (2) Identity foreclosures involve persons who have committed to parentally chosen ideological positions rather than self-chosen ones. (3) Identity moratoriums reflect individuals who are currently struggling with ideological issues. (4) Identity achievements describe individuals who have experienced a decision-making period and are pursuing self-chosen ideological goals.

Dan McAdams has applied the four identity statuses to research on religious identity in adolescents. In this research, identity diffusion includes those adolescents who have not explored meaningful alternatives in their religious beliefs, and who have not experienced a crisis. Identity foreclosure indicates adolescents who have committed to the religious beliefs of their parents or significant others but have not experienced a crisis. Identity moratorium means adolescents are in the midst of a crisis in relationship to their beliefs, and they have vaguely defined or avoided defining their religious commitments. Identity achievement indicates that the adolescent has undergone a religious crisis and made a commitment in religious belief.[34]

A Word on Racial Identity

Erikson has been particularly sensitive to the role of culture in identity development. Erikson points out that ethnic minority groups have struggled to "maintain their cultural identities while trying to blend into the dominant culture."[35] Erikson indicates that this struggle for identity within the larger culture has been the driving force in founding churches, empires, and revolutions throughout history. During adolescence, "most ethnic minority individuals consciously confront their ethnicity for the first time."[36] This renders adolescence for the ethnic minority as a special time period in their development.[37] The conversations with Mary, Ellen, and Kermit particularly indicate the process of racial identity development.

Tracy Robinson suggests that Erikson's theory influenced the research of other scientists who sought to explain how human beings develop psychosocially, cognitively, and morally. Although these theories provide a starting point for discussions of how identity develops, the unique realities of adolescents of color are not considered comprehensively. Robinson writes,

> An implicit assumption in each of these models was that identity is unidimensional, linear, and progresses in normative patterns, usually referred to as *stages.* Steeped within a modernistic tradition based on empiricism and monoculturalism, most of these stage models were developed in the 1970s and normed on white, middle-class populations, paying little or no attention to race or gender diversity.[38]

Racial identity is a single dimension of a person's complex, multilayered identity, which also includes sexual identity, spiritual and religious identity, gender-role identity, and other aspects of the total identity matrix of a person.[39] Racial identity development theory has been in existence since the early 1970s, with various models that included racial, ethnic, cultural, and biracial groups.[40] Robinson gives a review of several of these models, including white racial identity development. I wish to review William Cross's "Negro-to-Black" model and Carlos Poston's model of biracial identity.

In 1971, Cross developed the nigrescence model of racial identity.[41] The word "nigrescence" means the "process of becoming black" and describes the psychological model. Cross's nigrescence model was the "Negro-to-Black Conversion Model," utilizing a methodology based on self-analysis and participant observations. Cross's research took place during the Black Power Movement subsequent to the Civil Rights Movement. His research was conducted in his hometown of Evanston, Illinois, and in neighboring Chicago.

During the early 1990s, Cross presented his rethinking of the nigrescence model, indicating that the preferred terms for identity were now "black," "black American," and "African American," replacing the outdated term "Negro."[42] The intense renewed interest in "Mother Africa" ushered in the Afrocentric movement and a new look at the model. Nigrescence is a resocializing experience with the intention of transforming a non-Afrocentric identity into an Afrocentric one. The model has five stages and suggests that people progress through each stage based on their experience of cognitive dissonance at a particular stage. Considering the socialization of African American adults when they were children and adolescents, we see that not all persons are in need of nigrescence. Although nigrescence is not a process for mapping the socialization of children, it is a model that explains how black adults with various attitudes and characteristics experience transformation by a series of circumstances and events into persons who are more aligned with an Afrocentric worldview.[43]

The first stage is "pre-encounter," which focuses on the preexisting identity that will experience change. It can be characterized by three attitudes of the individual African American: "low-salience," "social-stigma," and "anti-black." Persons who have the low-salience attitude are not in denial of being black, but feel that this physicality plays an insignificant role in their day-to-day experiences. Black persons with the social-stigma attitude believe that their physicality is a disgrace that results in the necessity of negotiating occasional problems that their blackness brings. Persons with the anti-black attitude experience self-loathing and disdain for their reference group. "They look on Black people with a perspective that comes very close to that of white racists." Both social-stigma and anti-black attitudes view black people negatively. These attitudes may fuse with other pre-encounter characteristics, which include miseducation about the white race as the norm, the adoption of a Eurocentric worldview, and stress about assimilation and integration. These pre-encounter attitudes transcend social-class boundaries. The attitudes and related characteristics are found in blacks across the socioeconomic strata — lower-, middle-, and upper-class blacks alike. As with all the five stages of nigrescence, pre-encounter is "an attitude of perspective, not an inherited or divinely ordained trait."[44]

The second stage is "encounter," whereby circumstances and events that induce identity metamorphosis are determined. The black person experiences a set of powerful situations personalizing the encounter that raises his or her consciousness about racism and white supremacy. For example, events such as the assassination of Dr. Martin Luther King Jr. in April 1968 in Memphis, the Rodney King beating in 1992 in Los Angeles, and the brutal murder of James Byrd in 1998 in Jasper, Texas, caused rethinking about the problem of racism in America. Such thought engendered emotions such as guilt, anger, and anxiety.[45]

The third stage is "immersion-emersion," whereby the black person plunges herself or himself into the world of blackness, culturally, politically, and socially, and then emerges ideologically different. Blacks develop an insatiable appetite for black history, art, music, and intellectual discourse. "This immersion is a strong, powerful, dominating sensation that is constantly energized by rage, guilt, and a developing sense of pride."[46] The black person comes forth from the intellectual and cultural experience with new ideologies adopted during the immersion experience.

The fourth stage is "internalization," whereby the new identity is actualized, and the movement from previous stages resolves into reconstitution of personality and cognitive style. An Afrocentric self-understanding is seen in the articulation of a new worldview. The black person also begins to integrate the newly developed racial identity into his or her total identity matrix.

The fifth stage, "internalization-commitment," is an attempt to devote and extend a period or a lifetime to the translation of a personal experience into a plan of action. The internalization-commitment stage demonstrates sustained interest and dedication to the Afrocentric world-view.

Beverly Tatum argues that the first two stages of Cross's model of nigrescence are relevant for teenagers between the ages of twelve and eighteen. The pre-encounter stage of the adolescent is a result of the socialization that she or he experienced as a child whereby the beliefs and values of the dominant white culture are absorbed. Movement into the encounter stage is ordinarily "precipitated by an event or series of events that force the teenager to acknowledge the impact of racism."[47] The encounter stage results in heightened awareness about racism and the meaning of being a member of a group targeted by racist activity. Tatum contradicts Cross's research that the encounter stage occurs during late adolescence and early adulthood. Her research and that of Jean Phinney and Steve Tarver suggest that black teens may examine their racial or ethnic identity as early as junior high school. Tatum writes,

> In a study of Black and White eighth-graders from an integrated urban junior high school, Jean Phinney and Steve Tarver found clear evidence for the beginning of the search process in this dimension of identity. Among the forty-eight participants, more than a third had thought about the effects of ethnicity on their future, had discussed the issues with family and friends, and were attempting to learn more about their group. While White students in this integrated school were also beginning to think about ethnic identity, there was evidence to suggest a more active search among Black students, especially Black females.[48]

Tatum's own research on black youth in predominantly white communities concurs with that of Phinney and Tarver. She has found that environmental cues may trigger an examination of racial identity often in middle school or junior high school. Some environmental cues are institutionalized, such as "ability grouping" or "tracking" in middle and secondary schools. Although school officials purport tracking to be fair and unbiased regarding race, there is usually a recognizable racial pattern to how children are assigned. Racially mixed schools show a pattern of assigning black children to lower tracks rather than the honor track.[49] Mary commented on a similar situation in her junior and senior high school setting.

Cross's nigrescence model and Tatum's appropriation and critique of his work for the realities of black teenagers offer foundational theories on racial identity. However, theory on biracial identity is not adequately considered. The research of Carlos Poston offers a model on biracial identity development in adolescents. Poston reviews Cross's model of identity development for African Americans, Morten and Atkinson's "Minority Identity Development Model," and Stonequist's model of "marginality" as informed by Jewelle Taylor Gibbs's research. Poston begins his review on the models of Cross and of Morten and Atkinson, citing four problems that plague these models:

> First, these models imply that individuals might choose one group's culture or values over another at different stages. Second, both models suggest that individuals might first reject their minority identity and culture and then the dominant culture. Biracial individuals may come from both of these groups. Third, these models do not allow for the integration of several group identities. Self-fulfillment according to these models is based on integrating one racial/ethnic identity and accepting others; it does not include recognizing multiple ethnic identities. Fourth, all the models require some acceptance into the minority culture of origin, particularly during the immersion stage. Many biracial persons do not experience acceptance by parent cultures, minority or dominant.... In fact, many biracial persons often experience higher rates of victimization by parent cultures and other groups than minority persons.[50]

Poston's study continues with a critique of the first model of biracial identity development created by Stonequist. Poston argues that this model is a deficient model that focuses on black family pathology and the white family as the norm and reference point. Poston suggests that Stonequist's model for biracial identity assumes the problematic nature of identity development for "mixed race" people and views their adjustment and identity development as "marginal."[51] Poston writes,

> In essence, marginal people are associated with both worlds but do not wholly belong to either. This model suggests that mixed ethnic heritage serves to exacerbate problems associated with the normal process of identity development by creating uncertainty and

ambiguity in individual identification with parents, group identification with peers, and social identification with a specific ethnic
or racial group. Additionally, Gibbs suggested that dual racial identity can pose dilemmas for adolescents in developing a cohesive,
well-integrated self-concept.[52]

The problem with Stonequist's model of biracial identity, as critiqued by
Gibbs's research, is that it neglects the function of prejudice within parent
cultures and places the burden solely within the individual as one who
is struggling to determine a racial identity.

Poston proposes a more progressive model than previous models while
admitting that his model is based on a scant amount of research on
biracial individuals and their support groups. Poston uses Cross's idea of
reference group orientation (RGO) attitudes. RGO includes constructs of
racial identity, racial esteem, and racial ideology. There are five stages
for biracial identity development: (1) personal identity, (2) choice of
group categorization, (3) enmeshment/denial, (4) appreciation, and
(5) integration.[53]

Personal Identity

This stage consists of children who are beginning to place importance on
their ethnic group. Older children have a greater sense of ethnic identity.
Children's identity is based on self-esteem and feelings of self-worth that
they develop and learn in the family.

Choice of Group Categorization

Individuals at this stage are pushed to choose one ethnic group over
another as their identity. According to Beverly Tatum, this stage is
descriptive of early or middle adolescence.[54] The choice of ethnic group
is based on several factors, including (1) status of parents' ethnic
background, demographics of home neighborhood, and ethnicity and
influence of peer group; (2) social support factors of parental style and
influence, participation in various cultural groups, and acceptance from
parents and the families of parents; (3) personal factors of physical
appearance, knowledge of language, culture, age, political involvement,
and so forth. The primary choices probably at this stage are between
identity with majority or minority groups or two minority groups. For
example, an individual who is African American and Asian American

might choose to identify as Asian American based on physical appearance and cultural knowledge; status factors, such as living in an Asian neighborhood; and social support factors, such as acceptance by the Asian parent's family. This can be a time of crisis and alienation for the individual.

Enmeshment/Denial

Confusion and guilt characterize this stage of biracial identity because the child feels that he or she must choose one identity that does not represent the totality of the individual's background. People at this stage tend to experience feelings of guilt, self-hatred, disloyalty, and lack of acceptance from one or more groups. An example of this stage would be a biracial adolescent who feels ashamed, guilty, angry, and scared to bring a friend home because of the parent who has the racial background different from the norm of the neighborhood or school. Appreciation of both parents' cultures facilitates movement away from this stage and resolution of shame, guilt, anger, and fear.

Appreciation

This stage is the result of a resolution of the adolescent's shame, guilt, anger, and fear. The individual begins to learn about the multiple racial/ethnic heritage and cultures that make up his or her identity.

Integration

At this stage, individuals experience a sense of wholeness. There is recognition and valuing of their multiethnic and multicultural existence.

Poston's model of biracial identity, like Cross's nigrescence model, has a lifespan focus. As such, based on Cross's model, black adolescents are typically in the pre-encounter or encounter stages. This means that in Cross's pre-encounter stage, the African American teen is socialized into a racial self-understanding and worldview about the role of her or his physicality in daily engagement in society. This attitude can be located along the spectrum from low-salience to anti-black. Cross's encounter stage is that point where the black teen is caught "off guard" and thrown into crisis and reflection about her or his racial identity and worldview. The black adolescent in the encounter stage is in the process of racial identity transformation even though she or he has been socialized in a family that is race conscious. Ordinarily, this group is composed of black adolescents between the ages of thirteen and eighteen. Older adolescents who are college age begin to experience Cross's third stage, immersion-emersion. Biracial adolescents typically are in the stages of choice of group categorization or enmeshment/denial. These stages are character-ized by the biracial teen choosing only one racial identity from her or his total racial makeup. And having done so, the biracial teen eventually experiences guilt, shame, and disloyalty for choosing the race of only one parent.

Both Cross's nigrescence model and Poston's biracial model of racial identity development have themes of shame, feelings of unworthiness, guilt, disloyalty, and anger during those stages that locate most black and biracial adolescents. A teen expresses an anti-black attitude in Cross's pre-encounter stage, where her or his race is an imposition and causes disgrace and loathing from mere membership in the black community. The teen may perpetuate racist stereotypes or hold positive stereotypes of white people and white culture. African American physical features, such as dark skin tones, flat noses, full lips, and rounded hips, are causes of shame. This attitude is particularly debilitating for the black teen's self-concept, resulting in self-loathing, self-hatred, and a lack of self-efficacy. Biracial adolescents are located in Poston's stages of choice of group cat-egorization and enmeshment/denial. These teens also experience shame and feelings of disloyalty and guilt because they have chosen to identify with only one aspect of their identity, disavowing other aspects of their racial heritage. The shame of teenagers resulting from struggles with their racial identity implies historical questions that are the root causes for such debilitating self-understandings regarding racial identity. Specif-ically, colorism has a relationship to black teenagers' shame connected to racial identity.

Colorism is interiorized color consciousness among African Americans regarding skin color, shades of complexion, hair texture, and physical features.[55] This complex system of color grading — from black to brown to essentially white — often is directly related to social class.[56] White and light persons in the black community were allowed opportunity to advance by whites who controlled society politically and economically.[57] Mulatto persons were allowed to advance socially and economically through education and professional opportunities because they had the most Caucasian-like features. The term "colorism" was first coined by

Alice Walker in a 1982 *Essence* essay. She defines it as "prejudicial or preferential treatment of same-race people based solely on their color."[58]

Up from the Miry Bog of Shame

In Psalm 40:1–3a, the psalmist writes,

> I waited patiently for the LORD; he inclined to me and heard my cry. He drew me up from the desolate pit, out of the miry bog, and set my feet upon a rock, making my steps secure. He put a new song in my mouth, a song of praise to our God.

The poet describes a rise from the slimy, muddy depths of despair to the solid foundation of assurance in God, proclaimed in words of praise. A Scripture such as Psalm 40 is an appropriate starting point for a proposal to eliminate the tyranny of a "shame-oriented culture" regarding skin color and the toll it takes on the spirituality of African American adolescents.[59] Let us begin with a restatement of the meaning of *emancipatory hope:* it is the expectation of freedom from the dominating forces of racism, sexism, and classism, and the assumption of agency in God's vision for this liberative process. Colorism is an aspect of race and class domination germinating from the deeply inculcated ethos of what was considered to be acceptable and unacceptable skin color during the era of slavery.

Low self-esteem is the result of colorism among African American adolescents, particularly girls of dark skin tones. Lighter-skinned girls suffer the shame of alienation from the black community. I want to explore two very different stories from Scripture that illustrate overcoming shame. First is the story of Jephthah, followed by a story about Mary the mother of Jesus. I hope to illustrate the importance of honor overcoming shame as an aspect of a healthy spirituality.

Jephthah: A Gang Leader's Victory over Shame[60]

The story of Jephthah in Judges 11:1–11 gives evidence of risk factors for the making of a gang leader and his pursuit of honor.[61] Jephthah's early years are formulaic for youth gang activity. He was a Gileadite, from across the Jordan River, an area sometimes referred to as Transjordan. His poverty-stricken mother had been forced to become a prostitute so that she could take care of herself and, after his birth, Jephthah. His father could have been one of many men in Gilead. Jephthah was a poor boy, without any significant adults who accepted him. He was without property and the possibility of inheritance, even though he embraced these community values that ascribed honor. One's honor begins with the honor of one's family.[62] His family was without honor in the community. He grew up a tough guy, a fighter and a leader. He was a child on the margins of Gilead society. In fact, Jephthah's half-brothers, the sons of "Gilead's wife" (Judges 11:2a), drove him out of the city, denying his inheritance as a son of Gilead. He became a homeless young man, living on the streets in the land of Tob without a mother or a father. He was a warrior, and his charisma drew outlaws who followed him. They formed a gang, and they raided villages and caravans and "hired themselves out as mercenaries" for a living.[63] His reputation, and that of his gang, had spread for "being the meanest, most ferocious fighters the territory had ever known."[64] Neglect, abuse, rejection, and poverty are some of the complex set of influences that leads to his "lethal youth violence" and gang activity.[65]

When the Ammonites declared war against Israel, the elders of Gilead sought out Jephthah in Tob. They needed him as commander for their troops, someone who was a fierce fighter and who might bring his own regiment of soldiers. Jephthah, now an adult, was solicited to return to Gilead, after years of being banned from the city, so that he might assume the position of commander. "But Jephthah said to the elders of Gilead, 'Are you not the very ones who rejected me and drove me out of my father's house? So why do you come to me now when you are in trouble?' " (Judges 11:7). The elders evaded his query and promised him the position of leader over all Gilead if he would return and lead their army in battle. Hungry for honor among those who had rejected him, Jephthah tucked away the years of pain and accepted Gilead's, his father's, offer. Isn't it interesting how we seek respect from our fathers and others whom we venerate even when they have rejected us and never approached us until they wanted to use us? Such was Jephthah's situation.

The Gilead officials and Jephthah made their agreement before God at Mizpah. Danna Nolan Fewell writes,

> Jephthah should have turned them down flat. He should have laughed in their faces after the way they had treated him as a boy. But deep inside he wanted so desperately to be *somebody*. He wanted

to prove himself to the community that had never valued him. He wanted to have all of those things that that community had taught him to desire: a home, possessions, a place of belonging. More than that, he wanted to rise above the citizens of Gilead. He wanted to have those who had driven him away treat him with respect, with deference. He wanted to rule over them. He wanted the satisfaction of having them feel indebted to him.[66]

Jephthah's father, Gilead, denied him honor of the family name, of family property, and all the accoutrements pertaining thereof. Through rejection, Gilead created their son Jephthah the gangster. Yet in wartime, Gilead in desperation gave Jephthah, their son the gangster, ultimate honor: to become the ruler "over all the inhabitants of Gilead" (Judges 11:8b). Jephthah seized the opportunity to move from a scorned profession as outlaw to that of the highest-ranking official, from the economic underclass to the upper class, from the rejected to the accepted, from a nobody to somebody, and from the humiliated to the honored.

A Blessed Mother Overcomes Shame

Now I want to explore, from the opening chapters of Matthew and Luke, how Mary the mother of Jesus transcended the shame that affected her life, much as the transcendence of shame from colorism affects one's spirituality. As such, I suggest that a healthy spirituality transcends the self-deprecating effects of colorism and is actualized in self-worth, self-affirmation, and self-efficacy. Consider this midrash on Mary the mother of Jesus.

Mary the mother of Jesus is a good example of triumph over shame through self-affirmation and praise to God. Mary is a peasant girl from Nazareth, a town in Galilee. She is between the ages of twelve and fifteen, and she is pregnant. As if things are not complicated enough, she is not pregnant by her fiancé, Joseph, but by the "Holy Spirit" (Matthew 1:18; Luke 1:35). Joseph is a descendant of David and probably a carpenter by trade. At that time, for a woman to be engaged to be married but pregnant by someone other than her fiancé was an act of adultery, and the woman could be severely punished and humiliated. In years past, the law of Moses required such adulterous women to be killed. Although the implementation of the law was no longer as severe, the mental pain brought on by shame and humiliation was a type of death. Yet Mary was not destined for self-loathing. Nor was her circumstance the abyss of shame, because Mary was told by an angel from God that she was "favored" by God to give birth to the savior of the world. Being favored by God elevated this peasant girl to a place of honor. However, the angel had not yet convinced her of this lofty state. And so not long after the angel's visit, she journeyed to visit her cousin Elizabeth, who had been blessed with pregnancy in the twilight of her years. As Mary entered the house of Elizabeth, the baby of six months in her womb kicked as though excited. Elizabeth and her unborn son gave witness to the child that Mary was carrying as the savior of the world. Elizabeth's response to Mary's pregnancy confirmed what the angel had stated. Elizabeth affirmed Mary's pregnancy rather than humiliate her. As a result of the unfolding wonders in Mary's life, she gave praises to God for God's favor toward her, for honoring her to bless the world through the loins of her body. Throughout her pregnancy Mary, even though women whispered condescendingly about her pregnancy, moved beyond shame to affirm the honor given her by God, to strengthen her body for her delivery of a savior.

Conclusion

The stories of Jephthah and Mary are similar in that both of them overcame the shame of being marginalized in some manner, either for being the child of a prostitute or for being a poor peasant girl involved in a scandalous pregnancy. These stories are different in that Jephthah will go on to make a rash oath that eventually ends the life of his child. Jephthah takes the life of his offspring in the midst of moving from shame to honor (Judges 11:12–40). Mary, on the other hand, received honor as she carries and eventually gives life to her child, Jesus, the savior of the world. Jephthah's story emphasized how desperate a person can become in the pursuit to overcome shame.

Colorism is internalized racism about color that preferences skin color, hair texture, and physical features. This and related issues of racial identity result in shame, which in turn causes low self-esteem and low self-worth in adolescents of color. Colorism impairs the development of a healthy spirituality. The shame of colorism, which results in a sense of worthlessness, that one's physicality is flawed, shapes one's behavior toward oneself, others, and God.[67] The challenge to the Christian church is to help adolescents overcome the shame of colorism and the debilitating forces that dominate an adolescent's self-worth.

Notes

1. W. S. Carlos Poston, "The Biracial Identity Development Model: A Needed Addition," *Journal of Counseling and Development* 69 (1990): 152.

2. Susan Harter, "Self and Identity Development," in *At the Threshold: The Developing Adolescent,* ed. Shirley Feldman and Glen Elliott (Cambridge, Mass.: Harvard University Press, 1990), 356.

3. Pearl Fugo Gaskins, *What Are You? Voices of Mixed-Race Young People* (New York: Henry Holt, 1999), 12.

4. S. Fordham, "Racelessness as a Factor in Black Students' School Success: Pragmatic Strategy or Pyrrhic Victory?" *Harvard Educational Review* 58, no. 1 (1988): 54–84.

5. In *The Color Complex* authors Kathy Russell, Midge Wilson, and Ronald Hall discuss trends in church attendance among color-conscious congregations. Some congregations required black families to pass the paper-bag, the door, or the comb test. Ushers at the church door would require potential members to place their arm inside a paper bag. If the skin on the arm was lighter than the bag the visitor was invited into the church. Some congregations painted the door of the church the shade of brown required of congregants. Those with darker skin shades were not allowed in the sanctuary. In some churches, particularly throughout Virginia and in Philadelphia and New Orleans, a fine-tooth comb was hung on a rope at the front door of the church. Visitors whose hair was too nappy to pass through the comb were denied entry. Mulattoes and other lighter skin hues were readily accepted in these congregations. Although these qualifying tests no longer exist Russell, Wilson, and Hall argue that certain "black society churches" continue to be lighter than others. *The Color Complex* (New York: Anchor Books, 1992), 27.

6. Beverly Daniel Tatum, *"Why Are All the Black Kids Sitting Together in the Cafeteria?" and Other Conversations about Race* (New York: Basic Books, 1997), 52–53.

7. John W. Santrock, *Adolescence: An Introduction,* 6th ed. (Madison, Wis.: Brown & Benchmark, 1996), 107.

8. Ibid.

9. Ibid., 109.

10. Ibid., 108.

11. David Elkind, *All Grown Up and No Place to Go* (New York: Addison-Wesley, 1984), 28–30.

12. Ibid.

13. Ibid.

14. This definition of idealism is my attempt to collapse Santrock's definition of altruism (*Adolescence,* 435) with Robert Coles's definition of service in *The Call to Service: A Witness to Idealism* (Boston: Houghton Mifflin, 1993).

15. Santrock, *Adolescence,* 118.

16. William E. Cross, *Shades of Black: Diversity in African-American Identity* (Philadelphia: Temple University Press, 1991), 214.

17. Santrock, *Adolescence,* 331.

18. Erik H. Erikson, *Identity, Youth, and Crisis* (New York: W. W. Norton, 1968), 16.

19. Ibid., 117.

20. Ibid.

21. Santrock, *Adolescence,* 331.

22. Dan McAdams, *Power, Intimacy, and the Life Story: Personological Inquiries into Identity* (New York: Guilford Press, 1988), 215.

23. Ibid., 216.

24. Ibid., 215.

25. Erikson, *Identity, Youth, and Crisis,* 131–32, 142ff.

26. James E. Marcia, "Identity in Adolescence," in *Handbook of Adolescent Psychology,* ed. Joseph Adelson (New York: John Wiley and Sons, 1980), 160.

27. Ibid., 161.

28. Ibid.

29. Santrock, *Adolescence,* 334.

30. Ibid.

31. Marcia, "Identity in Adolescence," 161.

32. Santrock, *Adolescence,* 334.

33. Marcia, "Identity in Adolescence," 161.

34. McAdams, *Power, Intimacy, and the Life Story,* 218–23.

35. Santrock, *Adolescence,* 336.

36. Ibid.

37. Ibid.

38. Tracy L. Robinson, "The Intersections of Identity," in *Souls Looking Back: Life Stories of Growing Up Black,* ed. Andrew Garrod et al. (New York: Routledge, 1999), 86.

39. Cross, *Shades of Black,* 214.

40. Robinson, "The Intersections of Identity," 86.

41. Cross, *Shades of Black,* x.

42. Ibid., 189–220.

43. Ibid., 190.

44. Ibid., 191, 192, 198.

45. Ibid., 201.

46. Ibid., 203.

47. Tatum, *"All the Black Kids,"* 55.

48. Ibid., 56.

49. Ibid.

50. Poston, "The Biracial Identity Development Model," 152–55.

51. Ibid., 153.

52. Ibid.

53. Ibid.

54. Tatum, *"All the Black Kids,"* 181–82.

55. Katie G. Cannon, "Womanist Perspectival Discourse and Canon Formation," in *Katie's Canon: Womanism and the Soul of the Black Community* (New York:

Continuum, 1995), 71. See also Kathy Russell, Midge Wilson, and Ronald Hall, *The Color Complex: The Politics of Skin Color among African Americans* (New York: Harcourt Brace Jovanovich, 1992).

56. Emilie M. Townes, *In a Blaze of Glory: Womanist Spirituality as Social Witness* (Nashville: Abingdon Press, 1995), 101.

57. Ibid., 109.

58. Alice Walker, "If the Present Looks Like the Past, What Does the Future Look Like?" in *In Search of Our Mothers' Gardens: Womanist Prose* (San Diego: Harcourt Brace Jovanovich, 1983), 290.

59. Edward Wimberly uses this term to describe his own social location, where shame was overcome by testimony through storytelling about Jesus' triumph over shame. See *Moving from Shame to Self-Worth: Preaching and Pastoral Care* (Nashville: Abingdon Press, 1999), 13.

60. This story was first published as part of my essay "Hungry for Honor: Children in Violent Youth Gangs," *Interpretation* 55, no. 2 (April 2001): 148–60.

61. For this interpretation of the story, I use Danna Nolan Fewell's "The Children from the Other Side of the River," in *The Children of Israel: Reading the Bible for the Sake of Our Children* (forthcoming).

62. See David A. deSilva, *The Hope of Glory: Honor Discourse and New Testament Interpretation* (Collegeville, Minn.: Liturgical Press, 1999).

63. Fewell, "The Children."

64. Ibid.

65. James Garbarino, *Lost Boys: Why Our Sons Turn Violent and How We Can Save Them* (New York: Free Press, 1999), 13.

66. Fewell, "The Children."

67. Wimberly, *Moving from Shame to Self-Worth*, 16–17.

CHAPTER FOUR

"I DON'T SEE COLOR"

Female Adolescent Gangs

You will recall Kathy, a twelfth-grader whose theological motifs of resurrection and transformation were discussed in chapter 2. Her response to a question about hope was "Can't we all just get along?" which is a Rodney King ventriloquation that circumscribes her meaning-making about ending racism and violence. Kathy's response, like that of her peers discussed earlier, is not coupled with resistance language or religious language indicative of God's activity in ending racism and violence. When I asked Kathy a related question about her commitments to the liberation of African American people, Kathy replied, "I don't see color. So if I can help 'em, I'll help 'em. If I can't help 'em, I won't." By the words "I don't see color," Kathy means that race does not matter, that it does not determine her level of commitment for the betterment of people in general, whether black or white. "I don't see color" means that her actions are based on a color-blind view of society. "I don't see color" is Kathy's meaning-making about a color-blind point of view. Color blindness is considered a race-relations utopia where racial discrimination is condemned.[1] Kathy joins the chorus of both blacks and whites who argue that skin color is no longer an issue in human relationships of power.[2] Her belief in a color-blind society magnifies the harsh reality of strife between African American girls who posit a color-blind belief and those who do not. This chapter examines loyalty as an aspect of girls' spirituality among African American girls who associate within all-black groups or in racially mixed groups. The issue of color blindness related to a conflict between girl gangs is the starting point for this discussion.

The chapter begins with the life story of Yandell, who demonstrates a theological theme of care for her significant relationships and her hopelessness about the transformation of society. Although Kathy's concern for a color-blind world focuses the chapter, Yandell's concern directs a discussion of stereotypes associated with color blindness, as well as racially mixed girl gangs and the need for loyalty. The chapter concludes with a discussion of healthy loyalty as an aspect of black adolescent girls' spirituality.

The issue of color blindness and related conflict is even among Kathy's twelfth-grade peers. Yandell, another seventeen-year-old twelfth-grader at the Austin High School, is most concerned about racial conflict between girl gangs. Before broaching her concerns as a way of illustrating loyalty and conflict around color blindness, I share her spiritual portrait.

An Ethic of Sacrificial Care

Family for Yandell consists of her biological family — her mother, her siblings, and her two-year-old son. Her father, who had been separated from the family for an unidentified period of time, died of a brain hemorrhage. Her mother, who held the family together through the period of her father's suffering and final days, has been the pillar of the family. Yandell credits her mother for helping her "a lot." Throughout Yandell's pregnancy, her mother was present for her, and she was in the delivery room and was overjoyed to see the birth of her grandson. Her mother has been her hero through the family's hard times. Even though Yandell and her family do not take part in a lot of church activities, she and her sisters and brothers look forward to her mother lighting candles and placing them around the house during the family's special events. Yandell laughingly says that they often "bother" their mother about the candles. Occasionally she is a practicing Catholic, with her mother, during special holy days.

Yandell is a member of Common Ground, a parachurch organization. She does not regard the members of Common Ground as family in the way Mark speaks of his congregation as a "church family." However, as a participant in Common Ground's activities, she experienced gradual transformation in her life, much like Mark, Paul, and Kathy. Her transformation resulted from a friend's invitation to attend Bible study. After her initial experience, Yandell became an active member. Common Ground is very important in her life — its summer camps, Bible study, and especially the support and encouragement of her adult counselor. "It was deep. The Bible study teacher is deep.... She teaches us real well," Yandell remarks. She speaks warmly of her teacher, Cassie, who is white and is able to "understand what everybody's going through." When asked how she knew she had changed, Yandell responded,

> Because I do more for people than I used to do. I have always done [things] for certain people, but [now] I do more.... Now I give things to others rather than trying to get things.... She [Cassie] helps us understand the Bible. We sit there and read Scripture and she explains to us, she tells us, like, how, like in everyday life, like, how we live. She will give us, like, a moment where we can use this, and how we can use that ... and not to snap on things.

The most memorable moment for Yandell was during summer camp with Common Ground. Prior to summer camp, she watched her life gradually change. Summer camp was the climax of her period of transformation. Like others who stood and told their personal stories, so did Yandell. Telling their stories, singing, praying, studying the Bible three times a day, and asking "God to forgive us" brought her to the height of joy. "I felt happy, happier than I had been," stated Yandell.

Yandell believes that one can experience joy only by "having the spirit of God in you, the Holy Spirit." She credits Cassie, her Bible study teacher, for convincing her that prayer, giving your cares to God, will help you become worry free. She understands Jesus Christ as the ultimate example of one who confronted oppressive authority, which resulted in his death. In response to my question about unfair powers of authority, she said,

> Isn't that, like, why he got crucified? ... He always tried to do the right things. And they [oppressive powers of authority] didn't like it. And he was always trying to help people that were getting caught up. And they didn't like it. They, like, hung him. They crucified him.

Yandell understands Jesus as one who cared for people who got "caught up," and this resulted in his ultimate sacrifice, crucifixion. The theme of sacrificial caring is a theological motif in Yandell's life story and can be traced in the relationships she identifies as significant for her. Yandell's mother is her prime example of sacrificial care. She describes her mother as one who "cares for others." Yandell wrote this about her mother:

> My mom is the most important person in my life because the things she does and has given me are unlimited.... My mom helps me a

lot because I have a child, and she gives up a lot of her free time to stay with him while I work, go out, or just leave to have fun. . . . My mom also helps raise my little cousin and a friend of the family whose mother was on drugs. . . . Without her I would be lost.

Yandell's youth group counselor, Cassie, is another role model of sacrificial care. Yandell describes how Cassie sacrifices for the youth of Common Ground.

She helps us. She makes sure everybody who wants to go to college gets a way. She helps us with our research papers. We don't have typewriters, . . . she takes us to the south side and will stay with us all night until our papers are done and typed. And she will bring us home. . . . Like, if you have a family problem . . . like this girl's mother who had AIDS and died. The girl, Tricia, was pregnant. She stayed in her [Cassie's] house for a year until Tricia could get her own place . . . because her mother had died and her father was nowhere to be found. Mr. and Mrs. Cook, two other Common Ground counselors, kept her baby. . . . She [Cassie] helps people a lot.

Cassie and Yandell's mother demonstrate sacrificial care for Yandell. Perhaps these role models provided the pattern of sacrificial care for Yandell that she now practices since her conversion. She describes how she has changed: "I do more for people than I used to. No matter what they do, . . . I do more. Now I give things rather than trying to get things."

Another aspect of Yandell's spirituality focuses on a question about hope. This young woman, who passionately describes her Christology as Jesus' sacrificial care for even the least-recognized people in society, jettisoned her Christology when she talked about her hopes for humankind. Instead, she used apocalyptic language. She said, "I hope all these drug dealing and all the gangbanging stop. . . . I hope the world gets better before it gets too bad. Actually, it will come to an end because of the bad people." Yandell's concern about violence is echoed on another occasion when she passionately describes a violent encounter between opposing girl gangs. In the midst of this story are implications about loyalty among racially integrated girl gangs. Before I share Yandell's account of the altercation between two opposing girl gangs I want to discuss stereotypes relevant to the conflict.

Acting Black, Acting White

Teenagers on both sides of the color line harbor racial stereotypes about each other. Black teens hold perceptions about white teenagers' language, dress, and material values. When a black peer appears to demonstrate the perceived behavior of a white teenager, the black adolescent is labeled as "acting white." Beverly Tatum clarifies the term "acting white" through the work of Signithia Fordham and John Ogbu. They identified a common psychological pattern among African American high school students in the course of developing a personal and group identity as they become aware of racial prejudice and institutional racism against black people.[3] Fordham and Ogbu argue that this awareness leads to the development of an oppositional social identity designed to protect the black adolescent against the psychological assault of racism and to distance the white dominant group.[4] Posturing in the oppositional stance, black teenagers articulate their perceptions of "acting white" and the inappropriateness of such behavior among black teenagers. The point is succinctly stated in Tatum's quotation of Fordham and Ogbu:

> Subordinate minorities regard certain forms of behavior and certain activities or events, symbols, and meanings as not appropriate for them because those behaviors, events, symbols, and meanings are characteristic of white Americans. At the same time they emphasize other forms of behavior as more appropriate for them because these are not a part of white Americans' way of life. To behave in the manner defined as falling within a white culture frame of reference is to "act white" and is negatively sanctioned.[5]

In addition to adopting certain styles of dress and music, black teens who excel academically may be accused of "acting white" by those black peers who believe that studying hard and obtaining good grades is a value foreign to the black community. Fordham and Ogbu also discovered that of the black students who had been academically successful, few remained as such, because of the ridicule they received from their black peers.[6] Sophfronia Gregory and David Thigpen share stories of black teens who have been accused of "acting white" because of their academic achievements.[7] Shaquila Williams, a sixth-grader at Webster Academy in East Oakland, California, was accused of "acting white" and was threatened with the destruction of her books. Shaquila stated,

"They'll try and stop you from doing your work."[8] Shaquila's experience is similar to that of many other black teenagers ridiculed as "acting white" because academic achievement is stereotypically considered as a characteristic of the white society.

On the other hand, some African American teenagers are ridiculed for not being "black enough" or not demonstrating characteristics considered genuinely those of the black community. These characteristics include language, style of dress, and even choice of food. Judgment of a black teen as not being "black enough" is based on stereotypes held about African American ways of being. Labels of "not black enough" and "acting white" are used among some black peers as forms of resistance to racism.

Likewise, some whites teens ridicule their white peers as "acting black," based on stereotypes held about black adolescents. Some white teens hold perceptions that all black teenagers manifest a certain conversational style woven together with a specific voice intonation, a specific style of dress and hair, as well as certain material values. White teens have ridiculed their white peers as "acting black" if their peers are perceived as talking and dressing like black teens, as well as having a preference for certain types of music and dance, such as that identified with hip-hop culture. Research data on the "acting black" phenomena is sketchy. Only scant information about white teens referring to their white peers as "wiggers" has been reported on television newsmagazines and in other literature discussing race relations between black and white teenagers. The term "wigger" is pejorative, substituting the n in "nigger" with a w, stereotyping white teenagers who allegedly are "acting black." Rosalind Wiseman indicates that non–African American girls who emulate stereotypes of black girls are called "wigger" or said to be "acting ghetto."[9] Wiseman states that these labels are used among girls striving to meet racist standards of beauty; yet girls use these terms without any analysis or critique of their dehumanizing effect.[10]

The insult of "acting white" or "acting black" imposed on black and white peers, respectively, has been related to gang behavior and eventual violence. Za'kettha Blaylock, a fourteen-year-old girl from Oakland, California, who is academically successful, dreams of going to college and becoming a doctor. She is tormented, however, by a girl gang in her neighborhood. Za'kettha receives numerous menacing telephone calls, with callers uttering threats such as "We're gonna kill you." Za'kettha indicates that the threats come from a gang of black girls who specialize in terrorizing bright black students.[11] Similarly, some black teens might also refer to those white peers who affiliate with black groups as "acting black." A similar scenario regarding "acting black" and two opposing gangs of girls was shared with me.

Yandell described in great detail the violence among opposing groups of girls regarding a white member of one gang who allegedly was "acting black." This is to suggest that the European American girl demonstrated slang, dress, and gestures that are stereotypically considered common among African American girls. Yandell begins by describing the altercation. "This girl got jumped at school, . . . and, like, four really big fat girls stepped on her. And this was the most skinny white girl. . . . They said they jumped on her because she was acting black." Reflecting back on the incident, Yandell describes what had happened. However, as she continues, it becomes apparent that Yandell had a conversation with one of the groups prior to the altercation. She said, "Then one of their friends is white. . . . She just acts like one of them. . . . I said, 'How does this person act black?' I said, 'You are black, but you are acting white because that's how the white people, the slave owners act.' . . . So they got mad." Yandell was able to talk with the gang because of her own history. She had been in a fight when her gang confronted another group. "They jumped on me, and I got suspended," she recalled. Returning to the description of the altercation between the two opposing girl gangs, Yandell indicated that both groups had white female members. She pointed out that it was illogical to accuse the opposing white member of "acting black" when their member also "acted black." Yandell gives the gory details of the fight.

> So they jumped on the girl anyway . . . really bad. . . . She had no scars, no black eye, nothing. They just hurt the girl's back because they were just jumping on her. . . . They had this big crowd around them. . . . I said, "Why do you want to jump on her? Look at your friend; she's white too. And you're gonna stand there and say you're gonna jump on her for that? You might as well turn around and jump on her [their white member] too." They were, like, "No, no, that's our girl, our friend." And they jumped on the girl [opposing gang member].

Yandell has offered an account of girl gangs fighting over perceptions about racial behavior — in this case, that of a white girl gang member in a predominantly black gang "acting black." The events she described suggest a need for a spotlight on two interrelated phenomena: girl gangs and group loyalty among racially mixed groups of girls. I will relate loyalty to girls' spirituality by offering a history of girl gangs, focusing on the role of loyalty among gang members. I adopt Sudhir Alladi Venkatesh's meaning of "girl gang" as "the primary convention of street gang scholars to refer to collectives of predominantly female members engaged in social deviance."[12] He defines street gangs as "an organized social group governed by a leadership structure, having goals and means of obtaining them that may not be legal or socially sanctioned, and seeking to realize the interest of its individual members as well as the needs of the group."[13]

A Brief History of Girl Gangs and the Need for Loyalty

Anne Campbell, author of *The Girls in the Gang,* the seminal book on girl gangs, argues that girls were involved with criminal and conflict gangs as early as 1825 in New York City, such as the famous three-day feud between the Bowery Boys and the Five Points. These girls are believed to have performed the auxiliary role of providing needed ammunition and watching for weaknesses in the enemy's defense. Women were represented in various types of gang activities, from fighting to racketeering. Since girls were more commonly attached to male gangs as auxiliary partners, they were described as "sex objects" and used to instigate gang wars, provoke fights, and act as spies. In 1908, Carroll Terry, a dancer on Coney Island, gained her reputation as a "sex object" when she instigated a fight between Louie the Lump from the Bowery gang and Kid Twist from a rival gang. A series of violent events resulted in the death of Kid Twist and his friend Cycline Louis. In addition to being depicted as "sex objects," some girls were considered "tomboys." Battle Annie, a noted gang leader, used her prowess as a fighter to train other girls in the skills of combat.[14]

During the 1920s, females in the Chicago area participated in criminal gangs as affiliates of male youth gangs for the purpose of being sexual partners or diversions for rival gangs.[15] There were instances, however, where girls played dual roles of "gangster and sweetheart." An all-white girls gang, lead by the notorious Honey, was recognized as one of the few girls' gangs in the Chicago area. Honey had been known in the news-papers as a "bobbed-haired 'bandit queen' " who, at twenty-one, was the brains and sometimes the brawn of a crew of seventy-five robberies and holdups in the north shore area of Chicago. Among the other four Chicago girl gangs identified during the mid-1920s was an African American girls gang "having baseball as their chief interest."

During the 1940s, other Chicago area girl gangs were noted by W. F. Whtye (author of *Street Corner Society: The Social Structure of an Italian Slum*), particularly Italian girls in settlement house clubs.[16] In 1940, William Bernard described the New York juvenile gangs as being far more numerous than the sixty to two hundred gangs estimated by New York officials. He suggested that gangs were primarily "Negro, Italian, Irish, Jewish and Puerto Rican." He also suggested that in Harlem alone there were more than 250 gangs. During the 1950s and 1960s, W. B. Miller investigated two girl gangs. These were the Molls, an all-white Catholic gang of eleven girls whose ages ranged from thirteen to sixteen, and the Queens, an all-black gang of girls who were the siblings of the Kings (a male gang). The Queens ranged in age from sixteen to eighteen. They were not heavily involved in criminal activity, except for assault, and they also were less cohesive as compared to other gangs that Miller observed. In many ways, the Queens were more of a social club than a gang, con-cerned about dress, cooking, demeanor, and parties. With the advent of the Civil Rights Movement and the Women's Rights Movement during the 1960s and 1970s, girls' and boys' gangs were expected to participate. Many believed that they had nothing to lose by involving themselves in civil disobedience. "After all, gang members were alienated, poor, often from minority groups and had nothing to lose." It was expected that female crime would escalate due to the women's movement, but this was not the case. Both these movements had a direct relationship to African American girls in gangs.

Focusing on African American female participation in gangs, Carl S. Taylor's book *Girls, Gangs, Women, and Drugs*, and Deborah Burris-Kitchen's book *Female Gang Participation*, offer comprehensive historical perspectives on black female gangs. A related historical survey is Cheryl Kirk-Duggan's examination of the parallel societies of black sororities and "sistah" gangs in her book *Refiner's Fire: A Religious Engagement with Violence*.

In lower-class Hispanic, black, and white communities, teenagers give honor, loyalty, and fellowship as reasons for joining gangs.[17] John Quicker studied girls' involvement in Chicana gangs in East Los Angeles in 1974. He concluded that the gang came to demand complete loyalty from its members and also served as a family to the girls.[18] Loyalty in gang culture means standing up for your gang.[19] Considered as a cultural value, loyalty in gang culture is contextually grounded, which means that the gang develops the layers of meaning for loyalty.[20] This meaning is different from the general conventional understanding of loyalty to family, school, friends, and company. "Loyalty is grounded in the gang."[21] When a gang member reports to her "homegirls" that she was attacked by a rival gang, she expects them to take revenge on her behalf. Usually this means some violent response. However, there are instances when loyalty to the group supersedes loyalty on behalf of a specific member. For example, if a gang member commits a violent act that places the entire group under pressure from the community or police, group leaders might decide to jettison loyalty to a fellow member in order to preserve the well-being of the gang.

The Sex Girls, a late 1970s black and Hispanic gang with members in Brooklyn, Queens, the Bronx, and Manhattan, encouraged loyalty through its initiation rite.[22] A prospective member was expected to fight a selected full member in order to demonstrate her courage and worthiness. The intent of this initiation rite was to deter those girls who wanted to take advantage of the protection that the gang gives to its members without a willingness to fight for others. A girl who succeeds in showing courage and a willingness to be loyal to all members is selected for membership in the Sex Girls.[23] Within the Sex Girls there were individual loyalties for their male counterparts that sometimes led to conflict.[24]

The Five Percent Nation is a religious and cultural group of young women and men.[25] First recognized in 1976 by the New York police department as a gang, this group adopted teachings from the Nation of Islam. The Puma Crew is a female subgroup of the Five Percent Nation, whose founding leader, Sun-Africa, organized this girl gang at the age of twelve.[26] She described the group in terms of a "tremendous in-group loyalty resulting from jointly conceived clothing styles and shared activities kept secret from the adult world."[27] The loyalty shared among the Puma Crew went beyond typical adolescent girl rebellion to violence, drugs, shoplifting, and robbery.[28] The Five Percent Nation rejected the

Puma Crew for its rebellion against the "true" Islamic teachings. Within two years, Sun-Africa, the leader of the Puma Crew, started to align herself closely with the teaching of the Five Percent Nation, which included the basic philosophy of the organization and the "Six Rules of the Black Woman," both recited in catechism fashion.[29] Sun-Africa felt that she had matured and embraced the major emphasis of the Nation of Islam's philosophy—that is, moving "away from passive belief in a mystery god toward a self-consciously active role in creating a better future for black people."[30]

During the 1980s, the Black Sisters United (BSU), recognized as Chicago's largest federation of girl gangs, was organized. BSU's initial mission was to "mobilize and to provide goods and services for young women."[31] These young African American women committed themselves to confronting domestic harassment and social inequity.[32] As a girl gang coalition, the BSU functioned as a corporate gang, where primary goals and objectives were for financial gain.[33] On occasion, BSU members participated in deviant behavior such as street fighting and theft, but such instances were infrequent and, in the case of drug selling, individual forays into the underground economy were more common than any conscious attempt by the BSU to penetrate drug markets. The organization consisted of the top-ranking officers of various small sets of girl gangs in the Chicago area. These leaders were inspired by progressive and feminist writings, including those of Assata Shakur (the Illinois Black Panther Party leader) and Angela Davis. Many of these young women had participated in grassroots political movements addressing welfare rights and inadequate housing. Melissa, one of BSU's top-ranking officers, stated that BSU "was about empowerment." Revenue generation was central to the organization's efforts, thus pressuring its membership to increase income. During the end of the 1980s, the BSU became delinquent in its activities.[34]

During the early 1990s, drug trafficking became the dominant means of generating revenue for the members of BSU. Its leaders made a conscience decision to federate with the Saints, a male street gang, after some sets of the BSU started to affiliate with the group. The BSU disbanded during the mid-1990s due to "internal leadership struggles, differences in vision, and external pressures brought on by participation in historically male-dominated drug economies."[35]

Although the function of loyalty among members of the BSU is not explicitly discussed in the literature, loyalty is tacitly expressed by its leaders, Cynthia, Laurie, and Melissa. These women, each the leader of a member set, were with the organization during its formation and continued to be devoted to BSU until it dissolved. The leaders demonstrated loyalty to the organization, adjusting to the demands of leadership with the social and economic pressures imposed upon the organization. However, as indicated previously, the leaders were not able to keep the organization viable due to differences in vision, internal struggles, and the pressures of a male-dominated drug economy. The BSU was the largest girl gang confederation in Chicago from the 1980s until the mid-1990s. Since the early 1990s, other, smaller girl gang associations were formed by high-school-aged women who patterned themselves after the prominent BSU.

Scant literature on the topic hinders our understanding of the nature of loyalty among girl gangs, particularly among racially mixed girl gangs. The Sex Girls is the oldest racially mixed girl gang discussed by scholars. However, there is reason to assume that a significant number of racially mixed girl gangs exist today because of diverse and unpredictable changes in communities of inner-city youth, as well as the downplaying of ethnicity as the single indicator for identity. Ethnicity has little meaning among inner-city youth except "as it functions within a host of embedded identities that could get a young person somewhere in the immediate community. Being the local tough kid's younger brother, the girlfriend of a prominent gang member, or a player on a winning local ball team counted more heavily in daily street life than one's label of ethnic membership."[36] All of this suggests the likelihood of racially mixed girl gangs and the need for empirical study of this phenomenon.

In view of the altercation that Yandell described, how can girls exercise loyalty to the group while defending their ethnic/racial diversity in a nonviolent manner? How can girls transcend the borders of difference in the practice of group loyalty?

Girls and the Problem of Color Blindness

The preceding questions are specific to the altercation that Yandell described, and yet they focus on intragroup and intergroup relationships among girls. The questions also attempt to place loyalty and difference under scrutiny simultaneously. A broader and more appropriate question at this point deals with color blindness among girls. Adopting Patricia Williams's phrase, I formulate the question this way: Is there a color-blind future for black adolescent girls' relationships?[37] I give this response: It depends on the competitive influence of contexts that shape the racial ideology of girls, such as family, school, church, peers, and media. For African American adolescent girls, arrival at a truly color-blind ideology involves development of values, beliefs, and attitudes that are shaped by a sociocultural and sociohistorical environment that is void of legal and ideological discrimination. Presently, such a sociocultural and socio-historical environment does not exist. Even though black girls may feel that they are resistant to racial prejudice and can practice color blind-ness in their interaction with all people regardless of color or race, they live in an environment that makes such behavior extremely difficult. James Garbarino argues that our children are being raised in a socially toxic environment in regard to violence in North American society.[38] I would expand his argument of a socially toxic environment to include the racism and racial prejudice that are rampant in our culture as an aspect of the social toxicity. Not just black teenage girls, but all teenagers, are living in a racially toxic society where the practice of color blindness is extremely difficult. Where white teenagers must struggle with white priv-ilege when practicing color blindness, black teenagers must struggle with internalized racism. Ordinarily, adults who successfully negotiate all the stages of racial identity development as discussed in the previous chapter have the capacity to practice color blindness. Adolescents who defy the racial identity developmental theories have the ability to practice color blindness and reflect on its meaning.

Now let us turn to briefly consider the connection between loyalty and difference. Girls who matriculate within groups that are racially mixed, even deviant groups like the girl gangs discussed above, demonstrate loy-alty across the borders of difference. From relationships formed among girls in the Student Nonviolent Coordinating Committee of the 1960s and 1970s to present-day girls' clubs such as Girl Scouts and Girls Inc., there are numerous accounts of genuine loyalty that developed in whole-some girls' groups. Loyalty among black girls in racially homogeneous or heterogeneous groups directs our attention toward the aspect of girls' relational and spiritual selves and the role of loyalty.

Loyalty as an Aspect of Black Girls' Spirituality

An understanding of loyalty as devotion in girls' relationships is the launching point for reflection on loyalty and black adolescent girls' spirituality. A healthy spirituality for an adolescent girl "emanates from her relationship with God — the one she hopes will listen to her, value her, guide her, encourage her and protect her."[39] Additionally, her spirituality involves all the important relationships in her life that affirm the person she is becoming.[40] Black girls' developing spirituality is reflected through their relationships with mothers, fathers, sisters, brothers, aunts, uncles, grandmothers, grandfathers, play-mamas, play-daddies, and all other fictive kin.

Mrs. MacTeer, the mother of Frieda and Claudia in Toni Morrison's book *The Bluest Eye*, illustrates a stern but compassionate mother in relationship with her daughters and their friend Pecola. On the occasion of Pecola's first menstruation, Mrs. MacTeer responded punitively to Frieda by giving her several lashes with a switch after the nosy little neighbor, Rosemary, hollered that the girls were playing nasty. Mrs. MacTeer was about to whip Pecola when she saw the homemade sanitary napkin fall from under her dress. "The switch hovered in the air" as Mrs. MacTeer asked, "What the devil is going on here?"[41] Claudia explained that they were trying to help Pecola clean up. Frieda verified with nods. Mrs. MacTeer released Pecola, looked at her, and then pulled Frieda and Pecola close to her, burying their heads in her stomach. "Her eyes were sorry."[42] She gathered the girls into the house as she admonished Rosemary to go home because the show had ended. Once inside the house, Mrs. MacTeer took the "little-girl-gone-to-woman pants" from Claudia, and with the panties in one hand and directing Pecola into the bathroom with her other hand, she proceeded to wash Pecola and her clothes. "The water gushed, and over its gushing" Claudia and Frieda could hear the "music" of their mother's laughter.[43] When black girls have healthy relationships with significant adults, just as Mrs. MacTeer had with her daughters and Pecola, those relationships help their spirituality as well as other aspects of their development.

Likewise, loyalty among teenagers and significant adults shapes a healthy spirituality. The excerpt above from *The Bluest Eye* demonstrates loyalty among young girlfriends. Frieda and Claudia remained faithful to Pecola during her awkward physiological passage into womanhood. Particularly Frieda's devotion to Pecola propelled her to think critically and act justly on Pecola's behalf. Frieda's loyalty prompted her cause for justice.

Devotion or loyalty in relationships supersedes devotion to causes. In fact, devotion to a cause issues from devotion in relationships, particularly when we are concerned that those in relationship with us should flourish. This stands slightly in contrast to a definition of loyalty offered by David H. Smith. Quoting Josiah Royce, he defines loyalty as "willing and practical and thoroughgoing devotion of a person to a cause."[44] Indicating the centrality of loyalty in the work of twentieth-century writers such as H. Richard Niebuhr and Paul Ramsey, Smith states that loyalty is "an attribute of a fundamental relationship."[45] In response to the question of the object of loyalty, Niebuhr posits "a monotheistic god whose transcendence makes possible the integration of selves who see [God's] power in all things."[46] Niebuhr also equates loyalty with the inward passion that faith in the all-important "other" provides.[47] Continuing with his explanation of faith, Niebuhr states that faith is "infused as loyalty to a cause by others who are loyal to that cause. . . . Faith exists only in a community of selves in the presence of a transcendent cause."[48] My point here is to make the case that loyalty is relational, to God and to human beings. From the relational aspect of loyalty flows a girl's loyalty to a cause. Loyalty insists on devotion to a cause for God and humankind.

Loyalty is an aspect of black girls' spirituality when the welfare of those they are in relationship with takes precedence, when they are devoted to a cause in order that others may thrive. Loyalty of this kind is congruent with emancipatory hope and the type of spirituality that ministry rooted in this theological framework fosters. Black adolescent girls are loyal to God and humankind when their lives demonstrate devotion to the cause of eliminating economic, political, and racial domination. This commitment and act of fidelity to the cause of overcoming domination emanates from assurance and expectancy in God and God's promises.

Loyalty that is integral to black girls' spirituality can be illustrated through the life of Daisy Bates. This woman played an important and distinctive role in the dismantling of racial dominance during the Civil Rights Movement. Her loyalty to the cause of justice was seamless with her loyalty to the black community. Committed to the cause of school desegregation in Little Rock, Arkansas, and loyal to the black children on the frontline in the desegregation efforts, Daisy Bates became a prominent and important civil rights activist of the twentieth century.[49]

Daisy Bates was raised by her adoptive parents, Orlee and Susie Smith, in southeast Arkansas. She discovered at the age of eight that her birth mother had been raped and murdered by several white men. Her father fled Huttig, her hometown, for fear of his own life should he attempt to seek prosecution of the suspects.[50] Upon discovering the role that white terrorism and brutality had played in her own life, Daisy began to despise white people more and more. Noticing that her gaze disturbed a white drunkard when she looked directly in his eyes as he sat each day at the door of the town's general store, Daisy began a ritual of torment. She believed that he was one of the men who killed her mother. One cold winter day, after several months of having the upper hand for unsettling the man, she discovered that he was found dead in a nearby alley. A few years later, as her adoptive father lay on his deathbed, he admonished Daisy to redirect her hatred of white people toward the institutions and structures that caused humiliation for black people. Taking her father's advice, she later acknowledged that his admonition sustained her throughout her difficult years in the civil rights struggle.[51]

When Daisy was fifteen, she met L. C. Bates, a journalism major at Wilberforce College. Shortly after her father's death, Daisy married L. C., and they moved to Little Rock. The couple eventually started their own newspaper, the State Press, which gained a reputation as a voice for the black community "working for the improvement of social and economic circumstances for blacks throughout the state."[52] The Bates's newspaper catalyzed positive change in regard to police brutality and other concerns in Little Rock.

In 1952, Daisy became president of the state conference of NAACP branches, a responsibility that positioned her for national recognition in regard to the 1954 Supreme Court decision declaring segregation in public schools to be unconstitutional.[53] The ruling had been handed down by the Supreme Court in May, and the black community had hoped for evidence of desegregation in Little Rock schools by September. However, Arkansas governor Orval Faubus, under pressure from white supremacists, announced a plan that would not be effective until September of 1957.[54] The NAACP decided to challenge the school board's proposal for gradual implementation, a decision that catapulted Daisy and her "children," as they came to be known, into the spotlight.[55] The

Bates's newspaper recorded the many attempts by and denials of black children in the public schools from 1954 through 1957.

The "Blossom Plan" called for integration to start in the highest grades at Central High School, because there were fewer blacks in secondary school than in elementary school. In February of 1956, NAACP attorneys filed a federal lawsuit to gain the admittance of several of Daisy's "children" to white public schools at midsemester. The effort failed, as the federal judge ruled in favor of the Little Rock school board's timetable for integration on September 4, 1957.[56]

During the prior school year, black students were polled, and Little Rock school officials estimated that about eighty black students out of the several hundred applied for admission to Central High School. Of the eighty, school officials determined that only seventeen students were eligible. Ultimately, nine students became the "children" of Daisy Bates as this courageous woman protected these students throughout the ensuing ordeal. These students were Carlotta Walls, Jefferson Thomas, Elizabeth Eckford, Thelma Mothershed, Melba Patillo, Ernest Green, Terrence Roberts, Gloria Ray, and Minnijean Brown. Daisy shepherded the "Little Rock Nine" through weeks and months of potentially dangerous situations as they attended Central High School. Through her, the black community found ways to protect the teenagers from the vicious white mobs as they traveled to and from school. After a mob of angry whites attacked one of Daisy's "children," Elizabeth Eckford, because she had not received information to meet at the Bates's home and she went alone to school, Daisy got assurances from both local and state police of protection for the teenagers. Throughout the school year, Daisy Bates's nine "children" met at her home before and after school. She strategized for their protection and safety. Daisy maintained close contact with the youth and their parents, and she always advocated on their behalf at meetings with school officials when incidents occurred.[57]

A discussion of healthy loyalty in racially mixed groups of girls has been the primary aim of this chapter. Loyalty is viewed as an aspect of girls' spirituality. The life of Daisy Bates reflects loyalty as an aspect of her spirituality. Her commitment to the cause of justice because of her care for those in her community demonstrates this idea of loyalty.

Although true color blindness and the existence of a color-blind world are unrealistic, I do believe that fidelity among black and white girls' groups can be realized. Skin color continues to be an issue. For black girls, hair texture and physical features also are sensitive areas of concern related to relationship among mixed girls' groups. The ultimate goal is that girls will experience the fidelity that God ordains, and that this type of fidelity will encourage girls' healthy spirituality.

Notes

1. Ellis Cose, *Color-Blind: Seeing Beyond Race in a Race-Obsessed World* (San Francisco: HarperCollins, 1997), xxiv.

2. Ibid.

3. Beverly Daniel Tatum, *"Why Are All the Black Kids Sitting Together in the Cafeteria?" and Other Conversations about Race* (New York: Basic Books, 1997), 60.

4. Ibid.

5. Ibid., 60–61.

6. Ibid., 63.

7. Sophfronia Scott Gregory and David E. Thigpen, "The Hidden Hurdle," *Time* 139, no. 11 (March 16, 1992).

8. Ibid., 2.

9. Rosalind Wiseman, *Queen Bees and Wannabes: Helping Your Daughter Survive Cliques, Gossip, Boyfriends, and Other Realities of Adolescence* (New York: Crown, 2002), 90–93.

10. Ibid.

11. Gregory and Thigpen, "The Hidden Hurdle.

12. Sudhir Alladi Venkatesh, "Gender and Outlaw Capitalism: A Historical Account of the Black Sisters United 'Girl Gang,' " *Signs: Journal of Women in Culture and Society* 23, no. 3 (spring 1998): 683.

13. Ibid., 689.

14. Anne Campbell, *The Girls in the Gang* (Cambridge, Mass.: Basil Blackwell, 1991), 10–11.

15. Frederic. M. Thrasher, *The Gang: A Study of 1,313 Gangs in Chicago,* rev. ed. (Chicago: University of Chicago Press, 1936), 228, 240.

16. Campbell, *The Girls in the Gang,* 13–14, 20–23.

17. Irving. A. Spergel, *The Youth Gang Problem: A Community Approach* (New York: Oxford University Press, 1995), 97.

18. Campbell, *The Girls in the Gang,* 25.

19. William B. Sanders, *Gangbangs and Drive-Bys: Grounded Culture and Juvenile Gang Violence* (New York: Aldine de Gruyter, 1994), 24.

20. Ibid.

21. Ibid.

22. Campbell, *The Girls in the Gang,* 142.

23. Ibid.

24. Ibid., 153.

25. Ibid., 176.

26. Ibid., 203.

27. Ibid.

28. Ibid., 203–5.

29. Ibid., 216–21.

30. Ibid., 221.

31. Venkatesh, "Gender and Outlaw Capitalism," 683.

32. Ibid., 685.

33. See Carl S. Taylor, *Girls, Gangs, Women, and Drugs* (East Lansing: Michigan State University Press, 1993).

34. Venkatesh, "Gender and Outlaw Capitalism," 690.

35. Ibid., 686.

36. Shirley Brice Heath and Milbrey W. McLaughlin, "Building Identities for Inner-City Youth," in *Identity and Inner-City Youth: Beyond Ethnicity and Gender,* ed. Shirley Brice Heath and Milbrey W. McLaughlin (New York: Teachers College Press, 1993), 6.

37. Patricia J. Williams, *Seeing a Color-Blind Future: The Paradox of Race* (New York: Noonday Press, 1997).

38. James Garbarino, *Raising Kids in a Socially Toxic Environment* (San Francisco: Jossey-Bass, 1995).

39. Pat Davis, *Beyond Nice: The Spiritual Wisdom of Adolescent Girls* (Minneapolis: Fortress Press, 2001), 3.

40. Ibid.

41. Toni Morrison, *The Bluest Eye* (New York: Plume Books, 1970), 31.

42. Ibid.

43. Ibid., 31–32.

44. David H. Smith, "Loyalty," in *The Westminster Dictionary of Christian Ethics,* ed. James F. Childress and John Macquarrie (Philadelphia: Westminster Press, 1986), 359.

45. Ibid.

46. Ibid., 360.

47. H. Richard Niebuhr, *Christ and Culture* (New York: Harper & Row, 1951), 252.

48. Ibid., 253.

49. See V. P. Franklin, "Daisy Bates," in *Epic Lives: One Hundred Black Women Who Made a Difference,* ed. Jessie Carney Smith (Detroit: Visible Ink, 1993), 27–32.

50. Ibid., 28.

51. Lynne Olson, *Freedom's Daughters: The Unsung Heroines of the Civil Rights Movement from 1830 to 1970* (New York: Scribner, 2001), 134–35.

52. Robert M. Franklin, *Another Day's Journey: Black Churches Confronting the American Crisis* (Minneapolis: Fortress Press, 1997), 28–20.

53. Ibid.

54. Olson, *Freedom's Daughters,* 135.

55. Franklin, *Another Day's Journey,* 29.

56. Ibid., 29–30.

57. Ibid., 30–31.

CHAPTER FIVE

"I FACE GETTING PULLED OVER A LOT"
Racial Profiling

Mitch admits having a "hot temper when it comes to someone messing with [him] or [his] family." I expected him to tell me about teenagers or teachers in high school who teased him to the point of igniting his anger. Or perhaps he would tell me of episodes where a store clerk insulted his mother and he came to her rescue, returning insult for insult in a battle to save his mother's dignity. Mitch told of the ways he had cared for his younger brother who idealized him, so I thought that he would share stories of defending his little brother against a playground bully. But none of these scenarios followed Mitch's confession of having a hot temper in his life story. He said, "Me being a black man who lives in a predominantly white neighborhood with lots of Jewish people with a lot of money, I face getting pulled over a lot just walking down the street." This statement began Mitch's recollection of several incidents of racial profiling that he had experienced.

Some of the girls discussed occurrences of racial profiling against their boyfriends and fathers. Allie recalled an incident in which her father, a pharmacist, was pulled over by Chicago police officers who said that his car fit the profile of an illegal drug dealer. Terrie mentions the frequency of police harassment that her male cousins experience day after day.

Todd, a sixteen-year-old honor student who lives in Chicago's Austin Community, did not share experiences of police harassing him. Todd shared strong convictions about "black males becoming extinct" because of death from gang violence and high incarceration rates among young black males. In the midst of sharing his convictions, he stressed that "some [young black males] are trying to be good, are trying to be a better person, and have a good life. . . . If they run into trouble, it's because many people are against black men." Todd is not alone in his beliefs. Some sociologists and psychologists also argue that the young black male is becoming extinct. Todd's concerns are related to daily struggles of racism that young black males face.

In this chapter I focus on the stories of racial profiling experienced by some of the male youth. The racial profiling experiences and reflections of Mitch and Jason are highlighted. They are two teenage American-born Haitians with very different personalities, yet who both have dealt with racial profiling. I also offer two descriptive reviews on books concerned with ministry with black boys, lifting up that which is helpful along with my critique. Finally, this chapter addresses the moral agency of black teenaged males and its relationship to emancipatory hope.

Facing Racism Daily

Several of the teens discussed their daily struggles with racist acts perpetrated against them. Some of the young men talked about racial profiling against them. They did not use the language of racism or racial profiling, but they recalled stories in response to questions about unfair powers of authority that can be categorized as racism or racial profiling.

Seventeen-year-old Mitch, like Jason, is an American-born Haitian. He speaks lovingly of his maternal grandparents, who raised him, and openly about the problems he and his mother have experienced. He has shared a room with this grandmother and grandfather where his family of five has lived in a two-bedroom apartment as far back as he can remember. His grandfather cared for him as an infant while his grandmother and mother worked. After his grandmother retired, she joined her husband in caring for Mitch. Their close relationship facilitates open communication between Mitch and his grandparents. "It's easier for me to listen to them than my mother," he says. In contrast, Mitch and his mother have difficulty communicating about school issues. His grandparents have pushed him to be a good student in school —a challenge, Mitch admits.

His mother and father divorced when he was about two years old. Over the first eight years of his life, his father stayed in touch through letters and pictures from Boston before coming back to Chicago. Since his father's return, Mitch and his dad have had an on-and-off relationship. Sometimes his father picks him up on Sunday, and sometimes they talk by phone. Mitch's father has two other children, an older son and a young daughter. He has never met his sister. However, Mitch celebrated the first meeting with his older brother as the most exciting moment in his life.

They met through the efforts of his cousin. His brother "was trying to talk to my cousin, trying to take her to a movie," stated Mitch. He continues,

> She heard me mention his name a couple of times before. She asked him if he had a younger brother, and he said, "[Yes], his name is [Mitch]." And they had come over to my house one day, and he came in. . . . And she's, like, "Do you know who this is?" . . . We just, like, moved back and just looked at each other for about, it seems like, *an hour*. It was, like, two men staring at each other, and then he gave me a hug.

Since Mitch met his older brother, they have spent lots of time with each other on weekends, sometimes even visiting his father. Mitch is proud of his close relationship with his older brother, never failing to comment on their resemblance and similar characteristics. Mitch is proud also of his relationship with his ten-year-old "little brother," his mother's second child. "He's been my shadow since he was born," Mitch boasts. "I was watching him tell on me; he keeps me straight. It's not hard, but it's not easy taking care of him. . . . He sometimes wishes he was the same age as I was so that we could hang together. I still take him places when I go with my friends."

Mitch and his family are Catholic, attending church two to three times a month. He is also influenced by Haitian spiritual and cultural traditions, such as interpretation of dreams. Mitch recounted the event of meeting his uncle, his grandmother's brother, when he was fourteen during a visit to Haiti. Mitch described his eighty-year-old uncle as "more mixed" than his grandmother "because of his dark black [straight] hair and his gray eyes." His grandmother allowed Mitch to visit the family's old homestead for several days with this uncle. During the visit with his uncle, he was given "a very old book" to read that had been owned by his great-grandfather. "It was *very* old; the pages were just, like, crumbled when he went through it," stated Mitch. "He spoke Creole to me, and I spoke Creole to him. . . . He asked me to read it. . . . It was a whole bunch of sayings and proverbs and stuff like that, a whole bunch of prayers. . . . So it's a book of prayers to keep witches away and stuff like that. And it's also a book of interpreting dreams." Mitch read through the book, asking his uncle questions about the meanings of the proverbs and descriptions of dreams. He was particularly drawn to the dreams of "dogs biting you, and snakes biting you," because Mitch has dreamt these dreams before.

His uncle shared the family belief that they have the "sixth sense." Mitch embraces this identity and practices interpretation of dreams and other traditional family beliefs. He juxtaposes these beliefs with Christian practices of prayer and worship at church and at home. In fact, a very important time for Mitch as he prepares for a new school year is the ritual prayer that he, his mother, and his little brother pray. He states, "We had this thing where before we go to school, we pray the night before the day we go to school. We pray about trying to ask God if he could help through the school year, you know. We sit in a room, . . . read Psalm 91 out of the Bible. . . . As she [his mother] was reading, I felt weird, light-headed. . . . She said, It's probably somebody who was trying to talk bad about you or trying to hold you back in your school. We just released the bad." In the midst of telling about his family's prayer ritual, Mitch comments on the family's "superstitious" way that is connected to their Christian beliefs. Mitch points out that this "superstitious" way is connected to worship, funeral ceremonies, and All Saints celebrations at church. His devotion to family and spiritual beliefs, both Christian and traditional Haitian, forms the contours for Mitch's strong sense of identity.

Mitch remembers facing unfair powers of authority because of his race:

> I recall one incident when I was going to school early in the morning on Saturday because I had something to do at the high school. I left my house around six-thirty. It was still dark. And I'm walking down the street. . . . And there's no cars around, and I'm going to catch the bus. And I see two police cars over in the parking lot across the street from where I am. And I see one of them pull out, and I know he was coming to me. And I was, like — oh, man. You know, I'm getting ready. And he's creeping real slow to see who I am. . . . I had my hat and my hood on. And he couldn't see my face. I did that on purpose. I like messing with them for some reason, but I don't like them messing with me. So he takes his flashlight and he rolls down the window, the passenger window. He flashes

the light in my face while he's driving. . . . And then he puts on his lights automatically, and I'm thinking he's about to pull off some really bad stuff. And then he gets out of his car, flashes the light on my face, pulls out his gun, saying, "Freeze, don't move, . . . drop your bag." I had my backpack on. I drop my bag. I'm thinking this is routine stuff. I said, "What happened?" He said, "Turn around, put your hands on the window." It was raining. He tells me to take off my coat and my hat. He starts going through my stuff. He says, "Where you coming from?" I say, "I'm coming from home." He says, "Where are you going?" I said, "I'm going to school." He says, "On Saturday morning? Don't lie to me. What did you just steal?" He says, "What's in that bag?" I say, "My books." He says, "Come on, don't mess with me." You know, being very vulgar and everything. . . . A lot of cursing. Calling me out of my name, that's what I was waiting for. I didn't tempt him, but I was waiting for him to say something like that. And he started going through my bag, looking for whatever. He says, "You sell drugs?" I said, "No." He said, "You're lying about living around here." I say, "No, I am not." He says, "Let me see your identification." I had my wallet, and we just moved over there about three months ago. I didn't get my address on my license changed, and it showed my old address. He said, "You live over there, don't you?" I was, like, "No, I have just moved over here about three months ago." And me, when I feel threatened, I start laughing, smiling. And he said, "What're you laughing at?" I said, "Nothing." And he said, "I should take you down to the station right now." And I was, like, "I need to get to school." He says, "You don't have to worry about that, because if I take you down to the station, you won't be going to school for the rest of the year." I said, "What does that suppose to mean? I didn't do nothing." He said, "How do I know about that? How do I know you didn't steal nothing? I'm heading for the car right now and radio to see if anything's coming up." So he called down to the police station. He made me wait in the cold. He put my coat on his car in the rain. I was sitting there with just a shirt on in the rain. It was cold. He went in his car, sat down for a little bit; he wasn't doing nothing. And after a little bit, he grabbed his walkie-talkie . . . and he called in to the base, asking [had they] seen anything, did [they] get any calls from such and such district area. . . . And they were, like, "No, no call." And he was, like, "All right." He got out of his car. He said, "Here, take your stuff, go." And he wrote down my name and stuff, saying, "If I have any trouble in this neighborhood, you're gonna be the first one I'm gonna come to." I was, like, "You can come to me." I told him my address and everything. And then I walked about a block later. Here comes his partner that was talking to him in the parking lot. He asked me all the same things: "Where're you going? Where you coming from?" . . . I said, "Did your partner tell you where I was coming from?" He said, "Don't get smart with me." And he reached for his flashlight, a big flashlight. And my bag just dropped off my shoulder. He said, "What? You wanna fight me?" I said, "No, man, it's not even all about that. I'm just trying to get to school." He said, "You're lucky, because I'd have beat your ass all over this concrete, and nobody would have saw you or to even call my partner across the street to come and help me out." And he was right. If he would have beat me, nobody [was] in the street to see what was going on. I was, like, "God!" He was, like, "Yeah, go ahead." Then he took my information, my address, phone number, and name and all this other stuff.

When Mitch finally arrived at school, to serve his detention, he told his dean that if he ever got in trouble at school again, that the dean should not give him Saturday morning detention. He did not feel that he would be able to make it because of the long distance from his home to the school and the difficulty in catching the bus on Saturday. His dean expressed his sorrow about Mitch's harassment by the police, and he said that he would not give him anymore Saturday detentions if he got in trouble again.

This was not Mitch's first experience of police harassment and racial profiling. When his family lived in the prior neighborhood, a female cop patrolling the area would stop and search him "almost . . . every other day, for no reason. She would say, 'I heard several shots in the neighborhood. I'm just checking you out.'" Mitch said that his mother started getting fed up and asked a relative who was a lawyer to speak with her police chief. The police chief set up a meeting with the police officer on three different occasions, "but she never showed up, never. . . . I'd see her. She always stopped me, but then she would never show up for the meeting we were supposed to have." Mitch said that he and his family spent almost a year trying to stop the harassment. Mitch sees little reason why he should take down the badge number of a police officer who is harassing him. He has no faith in the justice system. Therefore, he feels that a black man filing a complaint about police harassment or racial profiling is futile.

Jason is an eighteen-year-old Haitian, born in the United States, who is a senior at Evanston Township High School. Jason's mother died of complications from diabetes when he was five years old. He remembers the details of her illness, and he again experienced the pain of losing her as he shared his story with me. Jason's mother took care of him and his older sister as a single parent. His father left their home shortly after Jason's birth. He feels that his mother's illness was complicated by her difficulty in understanding English, since French was her native language. Upon her death, Jason's aunt and uncle took him and his sister into their home, where he has grown up with their two children and two other cousins. The house seemed to become smaller and smaller as other relatives came to live for several months with them. Jason believes that his aunt's "strict" nature and very different disciplinary fashion were different from what he sees as more typical of North American culture. "She was raised such that if you did anything bad, you automatically got spanked. So she kinda exerted that same disciplinary action towards not only me, but also my sister and her own two daughters." Jason has a love/hate relationship with his aunt and uncle, especially in regard to his poor grades and his lack of concern to improve them. He acknowledges his poor academic performance, on the one hand, and brags about his sister's academic achievements, on the other. His aunt and uncle pressure him to do as well as his sister.

At the age of fifteen, Jason was diagnosed as having diabetes, after having been admitted to the hospital for an unknown illness. He "just wanted to stay there for the rest of [his] life" because of all the attention he received from the doctors. They inspired him, "gave [him] a direction to go with his life." Jason made decisions about his future at that point. He wanted to become a doctor, and he decided that he had to improve his grades tremendously if he wanted to reach this goal. Jason sought the help of his closest friend, who motivates him to achieve academically by competing with him. Another source of inspiration was a cousin who overcame obstacles to become a computer engineer.

During Christmas, Jason, a Roman Catholic, forgets his disagreements with his aunt and uncle and enjoys spending time with them and the other members of the family. The holidays begin with the special event of midnight Mass on Christmas Eve, where all members of the family are in attendance, as is required by his aunt and uncle. Jason admits that he likes Christmas Eve Mass because it is a time for the family to be together. On Christmas Day, the family gathers for a special dinner. Jason said, "I like it a lot because, you know, everyone from my family . . . all get together for a *big* feast." Everyone has to pray before eating. Sometimes, prayers might take "ten, fifteen, twenty minutes." "All the food is there. Everyone is looking at the table, and you can tell when it comes their turn. . . . They get kind of serious and tell what they are thankful for and what they hope for the future."

Jason clearly remembers his First Communion, even though he was in the second grade when it occurred. He described in detail going to the altar and the priest giving him "that little round piece of bread. . . . That was, like, the first time, 'cause before that I was never allowed to go up. Even if I did, the priest would bend down on my head and go, like, 'No, he cannot have it.' And I was, like, 'Why?' " Jason laughs as he recalls his response.

While talking about good and evil in the world, Jason states his belief that "evil can be an action that you do," and that evil is more prevalent than good. He concludes by saying that good and evil are "more or less related to . . . the Bible. . . . People have to search [the Bible] for meaning."

Jason is soft-spoken, and he is slow to respond to unfair powers of authority. He told of several situations in which he had been insulted or falsely accused by his supervisor at the video store where he works. Even during these events he demonstrated patient waiting until the crucial time to respond appropriately rather than spontaneous retaliation. Like Mitch, Jason has experienced harassment by the police. His response, however, was less resistant than that of Mitch. Jason described one such event as he discussed justice:

I think that, for one, that we [should] all receive justice, no matter what shape one comes in. I know for myself that I've been harassed by the [so-called] authorities for menial things that wouldn't even have been taking place had I been someone else. . . . I remember I was driving my bike in a predominantly Caucasian part of Lincoln-wood, and I was stopped. Twenty questions — ranging from why I was there, my name, my address.... I was stopped by a white police officer. And I think it was unjust, and that it shouldn't have happened. Had I been a Caucasian adolescent, that wouldn't have happened to me.... Basically, I answered all the questions. He asked me my name; I told him my name. He asked my address. When he found out I was from Evanston, he asked me why was I in that part of Lincolnwood. I said I was just riding my bike. And after all the questioning, he just told me how did I come all the way out here, how come I couldn't have ridden my bike somewhere else. And I was, like, I was on the bike and took a wrong path. He recommended to me that I should not take a wrong turn again.

Jason didn't pose any questions to the police officer when admonished not to take a wrong turn again. Jason believes that the police officer meant "that I didn't belong in Lincolnwood, or at least in that section of Lincolnwood, and that I'd be smart to leave quickly as possible." Jason continued, "I felt angry that I was stopped. But then I kind of rationalized that he's just doing his job. Then I was, like, no, that shouldn't have happened.... [I was] thirteen or fourteen. I then realized that I can't do anything about the way they think about me."

Black Males: Victims of Racial Profiling

Both Mitch and Jason are victims of racial profiling — that is, they experienced targeted policing efforts based on their race. "Racial pro-filing occurs when a police officer selectively focuses on a person's race, and subsequently follows, harasses, detains or arrests the individual."[1]In some instances, racial profiling has been trenchantly captured in phrases such as "shopping while black" and "driving while black" to describe more specific forms of racial injustice at the hands of the police. Sociol-ogists and criminologists have found evidence in recent studies of San Diego, New Jersey, and other locations suggesting that police officers dis-proportionately stop and search minorities. However, these studies only reaffirm what people have reported for years. How or why the police disproportionately stop minorities has not yet been determined through research. Ordinarily, statistical analysis is the common methodology for these types of studies, which yields quantitative data. However, this type of research only provides baseline data, whereas "racial profiling is a phenomenon that must be studied in conjunction with the question of why a person of color is stopped."[2]

The results of racial profiling can be fatal and result in massive civil unrest and rioting. Such was the case in Cincinnati, Ohio, after four black persons were killed by police in 2000. In Cincinnati, Timothy Thomas was stopped eleven times by ten different police officers over an eight-week period and given twenty-one citations. Eventually, Thomas was shot and killed on April 2, 2001, by a Cincinnati police officer. A total of fifteen black men have been killed by Cincinnati police officers in recent years, but no whites were likewise killed during that time.[3]

Since the 2001 Supreme Court decision in *Atwater v. City of Lago Vista,* racist police officers have the power to practice racial profiling more than ever before. In 1997, Gail Atwater, a white woman, was pulled over by a police officer in Lago Vista, Texas, handcuffed, and taken to jail for not wearing her seatbelt and not buckling up her two children, who sat in the front seat with her. The Supreme Court's decision determined that Atwater's custodial arrest was constitutional. This clearly violates the Fourth Amendment, which guarantees the right to be free from "unreasonable searches and seizures." With the *Atwater* Supreme Court decision on their side, racist police now can arrest African Americans, Latinos, Native Americans, and other nonwhites and never be required to provide justification for why they choose that course of action over merely giving a citation. Justice Sandra Day O'Connor wrote one of the four dissents, stating that the arrest of Gail Atwater was a "pointless indignity." A police officer operating with a racially prejudiced mindset might exclusively stop blacks and Latinos, as well as target them for maximum penalties.[4]

In 1996, the Supreme Court addressed racial profiling in *Whren v. United States.* The Supreme Court held that subjective motives of a police officer in making a traffic stop are irrelevant as long as the officer has probable cause. An officer who thinks, "I hate black boys, and I'm going to eliminate one every day," can pull an African American adolescent over and cite him with an offense carrying the maximum penalty. As long as actual probable cause exists, the arrest is legal. Together, the *Whren* and *Atwater* decisions "allow a racist police officer to act within the bounds of the Fourth Amendment when that officer's subjective state of mind in deciding to make an arrest is racially motivated."[5]

We see the consequences of racial profiling when racially motivated police officers are given carte blanche power to arrest black boys and cite them with offenses carrying maximum penalties. Racial profiling can be attributed to the alarming numbers of black boys in the criminal justice system. "The Sentencing Project and others have documented that as many as one in three, and even as high as one in two black men in certain areas of the country are under some form of criminal justice control (i.e., parole, probation or prison)."[6] Likewise, the California Post-Secondary Education Commission and the California Department of Corrections offer data for 1994 showing this 1:5 ratio: for every black man enrolled in a four-year degree program in California, there are five black men under some form of criminal justice control. In 2001, Steve Cooper developed the "one-tenth reality," which states this 1:10 ratio: for every black man graduating with a bachelor's degree from a public college or university in California, there are ten black men sentenced to prison with a felony conviction. By contrast, for white men there is this 1.1:1 ratio: for just over every one white man who will graduate from a public college or university in California, there is only one white man sentenced to prison with a felony conviction.[7] These statistics from California reflect a trend among black males that has been prevalent throughout the United States since the 1980s. Black men make up close to 6 percent of the U.S. population, yet the number of black males in prison exceeds the number of black males in college.[8] Homicide is the leading cause of death among young black men, accounting for approximately 20 percent of the deaths in black males between the ages of fifteen and twenty-five.[9]

Although these high rates of incarceration and homicide among young black males are not directly correlated to racial profiling, research on these phenomena implies a connection. The research of criminologists and sociologists examining the causes of disproportionate minority incarcerations and homicides has hypothesized racial profiling as an explanation.[10]

Saving Black Sons

Racial profiling is one aspect of the broader problem of racism and racist acts that confront the black male adolescent. Research is scant regarding racial profiling among black boys. However, some related theories have been offered by black psychologists, such as Jawanza Kunjufu. I offer a descriptive review and critique of two of Kunjufu's books, *Countering the Conspiracy to Destroy Black Boys,* volumes 1 and 2, because they frequently are used to form curricular materials and rites of passage programs for boys in a multitude of churches. In these books he argues that there is an intentional plot to destroy black boys in the United States. This conspiracy is complex and interwoven, including advocates of white supremacy and promoters of drug use and gang violence, as well as apathetic and indifferent parents and educators, and white liberals who deny their own racism.[11]

Focusing on the context of the school, Kunjufu suggests that the conspiracy against African American males becomes evident prior to the transitional period from primary to intermediate divisions in school. He calls this "the fourth grade failure syndrome," where black boys become increasingly unenthusiastic about school and begin a downward spiral academically. Citing educator Harry Morgan, Kunjufu argues that the syndrome is due to a combination of things, including the individually competitive classroom environments that supplant the preferable socially interactive learning environments. Kunjufu also identifies "male seasoning" as another aspect of conspiracy against black boys. Male seasoning is a dehumanization process of indoctrinating black boys against themselves — a conspiracy designed to make black boys skeletons, with no feelings and compassion for their future children, for women, or for their male peers. It is the socialization and indoctrination of boys whereby they take on the myths of "real men." The mythical characteristics of manhood include these: real men never cry; real men do not need to see a doctor; real men "bring home the bacon"; and real men do not display affection to other males. "The poor communication skills, decline in academic interests, and weak emotional development may be linked to the male seasoning process."[12]

Parents are considered the main perpetuators of male seasoning, by parenting black boys in ways that render them economically, emotionally, and domestically insufficient. Kunjufu says that this type of parenting "fits the sexist mold" whereby the male child is reared with little or no household responsibilities, such as cooking or cleaning. By contrast, the female child is raised with household skills. Parents and educators are guilty, Kunjufu continues, of not encouraging the black male child to be interested in arts, religion, and reading. This sexist child-rearing practice is captured in the popular saying "Mothers raise their daughters and love their sons," which means that girls are "raised" to be self-sufficient, while boys are "loved" into dependency and given little or no expectations, conditions, or responsibilities.[13]

Kunjufu seeks to pinpoint why, when, and how African American boys are denied the skills necessary for manhood and to suggest strategies that can help negate the conspiracy and enhance African American male development.[14] The goal of the black community, Kunjufu suggests, is to help black boys make a successful transition from boyhood to manhood. He argues that the conspiracy against black boys will continue until African American women admit that only men can make boys into men, and African American men become responsible for giving direction or mentoring at least one male child.

Kunjufu's proposal that black males should mentor black boys to end the conspiracy against boys means mentoring one-on-one as well as a variety of men mentoring one boy. Kunjufu cites his own experience as an example. In addition to having a very supportive father, he also credits his high school track coach for inspiring him to improve his failing grades and to persevere when he faced difficulties.[15] Additionally, Kunjufu credits a male peer for encouraging him during a period of indecisiveness in his career. The mandate for black men to mentor black boys, as Kunjufu's experience suggests, means black men of integrity engaging in quality time with boys rather than only athletic and political celebrities being sought as mentors for black boys. His list of practical suggestions for ending the conspiracy against black boys includes more black male teachers in elementary and junior high school, methods to help boys resolve conflicts constructively, incentives for academic excellence targeting black boys, and other ideas involving parents and extended family members. Based on his own experience, Kunjufu suggests that extended family members should expose black boys to "the dangers of the street" through reality field trips to drug abuse treatment centers, jails, and hospital emergency rooms on Friday or Saturday nights. Finally, he suggests forming a coalition among black parents, male mentors, and educators to confront violence from street gangs.[16]

In volume 2 of *Countering the Conspiracy to Destroy Black Boys,* Kunjufu continues to provide more information to parents, female teachers, and male community activists regarding the development of black boys into manhood. He suggests practical ways of helping black boys become responsible in all contexts of their lives, including responsibilities in the home. Here, Kunjufu revisits male seasoning, specifically arguing that black mothers handicap their sons by not training them to be domestically responsible. He contends that mothers lack knowledge of masculinity. Negatively, he suggests that black mothers feel that domestic activities such as washing dishes or house cleaning are feminine responsibilities and may lead to homosexuality.[17] This is one of five indictments against black mothers in regard to male seasoning.

Kunjufu also suggests that female teachers, both black and white, have a negative influence on the academic success of black boys. He correlates the fact that the majority of teachers are female with the disproportionately high rates of Educable Mentally Retarded (EMR) and Behavioral Disorders (BD) among black boys. Kunjufu also correlates academic failure among black boys with the residual effects of female teachers who have experienced psychological or physical abuse from significant men in their lives. Additionally, he argues that white female teachers who have never encountered black boys in their classrooms cannot teach them, because they do not understand them. Kunjufu offers a litany of issues regarding females who teach black boys, including how a female teacher feels about herself; when a black boy looks at her defiantly; how a female teacher feels about men; where she is located on the continuum between "traditional" wife and "lesbian"; what her exposure to black culture has been; and when she sees a black boy, whether she sees a future political leader or a drug addict.[18] Kunjufu maintains that the encounter between black boys and female teachers results in a series of inappropriate actions, including hollering at the student or an exchange of hollering, the student's eventual placement in EMR or other special-education classes, and other "showdowns" between the black male student and the female teacher.[19] Ultimately, if black boys are to succeed academically, Kunjufu insists, female teachers must develop curricula that address their specific culture and way of being. Such curricula include attention to their shorter attention span, the influence of peers, more interest in mathematics than reading, and emphasis on oral traditions such as playing the dozens, signifying, and rapping.

In both volumes 1 and 2 of *Countering the Conspiracy to Destroy Black Boys,* Kunjufu proposes an organization called "Simba," which in Swahili means "young lion," for the purpose of bringing black boys to manhood while being mentored by black men. The ultimate goal of Simba is to prepare black boys for the rite of passage into manhood assisted solely by black men. Each boy is matched with a man who serves as a role model. Simba programs usually serve black boys between the ages of seven and nineteen.[20] In addition to Simba rites of passage programs Kunjufu recommends *The Orita for Black Youth,* by Frank Fair, and Nathan and Julia Hare's *The Passage.*

Throughout volumes 1 and 2, Kunjufu criticizes the church and women. His critique of the church is that it fails to assist young boys in the passage to manhood. He argues that the "church has not been able to capture the minds of our youth."[21] He continues to admonish black churches to examine the reasons why youth, specifically male youth, have not been attracted to the church. He also criticizes the black church for failing to give positive role models to black boys. He suggests a collaboration between the church and the extended families of boys. Additionally, he suggests that churches examine the Nation of Islam and its success with black boys.

Although Kunjufu repeatedly disclaims the intent to blame mothers, female teachers, or other women for their inability to help boys attain manhood, he continuously indicts women in the lives of black boys. Kunjufu contradicts himself on this account. He writes, "I sincerely believe that only men can develop boys into men."[22] As we saw, Kunjufu accuses women of hindering the passage to manhood for black boys in a variety of settings, from the home to the school. By strongly suggesting that women are responsible for male seasoning, for tracking black boys into "special education" classes, and for other forms of academic failure, Kunjufu reveals himself to be sexist and patriarchal.

Additionally, Kunjufu weaves homophobic statements throughout volumes 1 and 2 of *Countering the Conspiracy to Destroy Black Boys.* He implies that the rise in the number of gay males can be attributed to mothers socializing their sons without male role models. He even suggests that lesbians, particularly lesbian teachers, have an inverse effect on the passage into manhood for boys. He also makes irresponsible statements suggesting that homosexuality in boys and girls is directly related to parenting. He argues that the "swelling number of homosexual men" is a result of the absence of fathers and significant men in the lives of boys, or of the failure of those men who are present in the lives of boys to show compassion to them. He illustrates his point with a story of a father embarrassed by his son's failure at baseball while the father's colleagues were watching. The father did not talk to his son for a week and was too embarrassed to go to the office. Kunjufu argues that the son probably suffered "irreparable damage, making him a prime candidate for homosexuality." Another irresponsible argument is that the male "macho" image, particularly in cases of sexual abuse, is a leading contributor to lesbianism.[23] Although Kunjufu's basic premise —black boys need assistance into manhood from role models and mentors —has merit, his argument is sexist and homophobic.

African American ethicist and theologian Robert M. Franklin also has offered practical suggestions for saving black boys. A brief descriptive review of his book *Another Day's Journey* offers insights into the African American church since the Civil Rights Movement, including a description of the culture and spiritualities of the contemporary black church. In setting the context for reflection on the status of the black church since the 1960s, Franklin shares autobiographical information. Using the tragedy of the assassination of Dr. Martin Luther King Jr., Franklin launches his coming-of-age story.[24] His ecology of family, church, and school provided the foundation for fashioning him into a public theologian. In a subsequent chapter on youth, Franklin credits his ecology for helping him survive the urban terrain of Chicago: "I know that I could not have survived without the support and love of an extended family, an engaging church, a network of caring neighbors, and mission-driven public school teachers and administrators."[25] As Franklin draws his autobiographical reflections to a close, he writes,

> By lifting up some of the salient moments of my life, I hope to remind readers that there are young black males from working-class, inner-city families and Pentecostal churches who stand ready to contribute to the betterment of the church and the larger society. In one sense, my story also underscores that certain experiences work constructively to direct the boundless energies of youth. Church involvement, part-time employment, rewards for intellectual performance, protection from negative influences in the community, and travel beyond one's village all work. We need more, not less, of these opportunities.[26]

Franklin's reflections on his life story set the stage for his concern to save today's youth, particularly poor African American urban males. Citing literature and statistics, Franklin argues that society views inner-city black males in a variety of negative ways, such as the "lost generation" and "superpredators." Franklin believes that "the core crisis that these wasted treasures face is *spiritual.*"[27] By "spiritual," he means "a person's sense of identity in relation to other people and to God," whereby a young man is grounded in basic values, moral commitments, and the capacity to engage in ethical reasoning. Franklin does not hold black boys solely responsible for their crisis in spiritual identity. He points to urban economic and political realities that limit their opportunities for employment. At the same time, he argues that these "prodigal sons are responsible for how they respond to, and manage, the hand that life has dealt." Referencing *The Black Church in the African American Experience,* by C. Eric Lincoln and Lawrence H. Mamiya, Franklin indicates the failure of churches to provide ministries that address the problems that youth face and also engage them constructively.[28] Churches fail to provide effective and engaging ministries for both churched and unchurched black youth.

In addition to identifying a spiritual identity crisis, Franklin also cautiously argues that there is a crisis of institutional participation by black males that has been historically significant for socializing them. These institutions include school, family, and church. Franklin's 1977 research, which examines gender inequality in churches, suggests institutional and personal factors for black men leaving the church. Franklin's more recent research points to black males returning to the church, and thus their number now equaling that of women. Franklin contends that anecdotal evidence indicates that black males are returning to the church because they have incorporated "positive characteristics typical of black churches before the civil rights movement," such as prophetic preaching and empowering educational ministry. Although there are congregations attracting large numbers of black males, he points out that "the renewed congregations appeal to upwardly mobile, well-educated men with middle-class aspirations. The churches continue to be less attractive to men in the underclass who feel little loyalty to conventional economic structures, cultural values, family norms, and political and educational systems."[29]

Additionally, Franklin discusses the Million Man March, calling it "an extraordinary expression of personal and collective moral renewal by the nation's most enigmatic and often threatening portion of the population."[30] He discusses four lessons that he learned from his experience of the Million Man March:

1. Men from a variety of backgrounds can gather for religious and politically constructive purposes.

2. Revitalization of economically, socially, and politically oppressed communities can occur through Christian and Muslim collaborative efforts.

3. Single-gender gatherings may be inadequate for constructing male-female partnerships focused on reconciliation and community development.

4. Leaders on the edge of the black community who attempt worthy projects lack authority or influence necessary for mobilization and participation of the larger community.[31]

Franklin concludes his chapter on "redeeming prodigal youth" (the chapter's subtitle) by suggesting a list of successful youth programs. Citing educator Benjamin Canada, Franklin affirms that youth programs that mentor, monitor, and minister to youth are the most effective. Such programs provide significant adult relationships for youth, track performance of youth in both academic settings and the labor force, and offer educational ministries that inculcate values and self-love as well as "provide care and discipline from a religious perspective." Franklin writes, "Despite the challenges young black males face, the good news is that they can be redeemed, as can all young people who have gone the way of the biblical prodigal son." He suggests that those men who are aware of the situations confronting urban males and are willing "to act as moral agents, not passive victims" are a sign of hope.[32]

Franklin has sufficiently identified the problem among some black male youth: they lack a spiritual identity and are nonparticipants in traditionally significant black institutions. This is especially true among inner-city black boys who have been labeled as superpredators and described as gangbangers, drug dealers, and preteen assassins who are "radically impulsive and brutally remorseless."[33] However, I am concerned that his proposal of mentoring, monitoring, and ministering to black male youth does not offer hope to all black boys, including those labeled as superpredators living in poverty. Franklin has rightly argued that the current growing numbers of black males attracted to the church and its programs are predominantly middle class. These are the same youth participating in the mentoring, monitoring, and ministering that

Franklin lifts up. He does not offer ways that the church can reach out to black boys identified by sociologists as superpredators. What are the Protestant black church programs that have been transformative in the lives of boys in violent gangs? Also, although programs that mentor our black sons have merit, the monitoring aspect of Franklin's proposal is problematic. Monitoring should include more than the academic and job performance of black boys. These two variables fail to capture the holistic nature of a black boy in the process of becoming a man. Other variables should be added to this tracking research, including acts of service; leadership in nonprofit institutions, such as the church; and school and recreational institutions, such as the YMCA. Also, it is unclear what objective tracking of the performance of black boys will accomplish. Perhaps, statistics resulting from monitoring performance of black boys would serve the purpose of dispelling myths or inaccurate statistics in sociological and psychological journals that tend to paint mental images of pathological black boys or boys functioning at a social deficit.

The ministering component of the program — the specific values, discipline, and care that a congregation can provide — is not mutually exclusive of the mentoring component. It would be helpful to see a more developed understanding of the ministering component or a use of it as an umbrella to capture the whole enterprise as ministry to black boys. I agree with Franklin when he states, "Ministry is the church's response to the extravagant love and grace of God."[34] This is precisely why the youth ministry model of mentoring, monitoring, and ministering should be recast under the broader theological understanding of ministry. Finally, Franklin does not provide the track record of his mentoring, monitoring, and ministering program. It would be helpful to see empirical data that supports the success of this program.

In an earlier chapter Franklin illustrates his idea of politically empowering religious education in faith communities that nurture hope by citing Jawanza Kunjufu. Franklin lifts up Kunjufu's idea of "coaches" to connote the ability to integrate subject matter and learning styles with development of identity and self-esteem in black boys. Franklin continues, "In black churches, the most effective teachers are coaches whose involvement in a child's character development may exceed that of the parent."[35] Franklin offers Kunjufu's idea of coaches without giving an honest critique of the sexist and homophobic context in which Kunjufu's idea is couched. Kunjufu is suggesting heterosexual black men as the only guarantors for helping black boys become healthy and whole adults. The coach metaphor is "genderized," implying a male adult. Also, good teachers in educational ministry, regardless of the metaphor used to describe them, use integrative pedagogical processes as they view Christian faith formation holistically — not just for the head, but intellectually, physically, socially, and spiritually. To conclude: Franklin has raised some important sociological and spiritual issues in regard to saving black boys from urban plight; however, his models and programs are inadequate for saving our black sons, particularly inner-city poor boys, who face enormous challenges to survive.

I have given lengthy descriptive reviews of Kunjufu's *Countering the Conspiracy to Destroy Black Boys* (volumes 1 and 2) and Franklin's *Another Day's Journey* in an effort to discover how black boys are to confront racism and racist acts, particularly racial profiling. I chose Kunjufu's volumes because of their popularity in African American churches for developing ministries for black boys. Although empirical data does not support the use of Kunjufu's volumes in structuring youth programs (see Lincoln and Mamiya, *The Black Church in the African American Experience*), anecdotal information does support such a use. I chose Franklin's book because it is one of the few recently published books that looks at problems of black boys coming of age in the United States through the eyes of a theologian and ethicist.

Neither Kunjufu nor Franklin offers insightful information regarding the formation of black boys as moral agents against racist acts perpetrated against them, particularly racial profiling. The remaining pages of the chapter will address this problem from the perspective of emancipatory hope — the expectation that God's promises are true, that racial domination and other dehumanizing hegemonic forces will be toppled, and that youth have agency in God's dismantling process. I want to examine briefly the moral agency of black boys and a way of meaning-making when confronting racial profiling.

The Moral Agency of Black Boys

The moral agency of black male teenagers is central to a ministry for emancipatory hope. Moral agency, as I conceive it, is the means of action through which one ascertains that which is good and right for oneself and for others. Moral agency depends on an understanding of morality. Peter

Paris offers a definition of morality in conjunction with his understanding of moral agency: "Morality is expressive of the capacity to determine the quality of human activity by making choices in accordance with understandings of good and bad, right and wrong. As moral agents, human beings are able to perceive others as subjects, and in their encounter with them they may choose to treat them either as subjects or as objects. Similarly, all human beings claim rights that obligate others to respect their dignity as subjects."[36] Hence, moral agency is human activity or human action whereby decisions are made so that self and others are subjects rather than objects.

African American male adolescents are moral agents when they seek to make decisions that enable their humanity and the humanity of others. They are moral agents when they seek to be subjects and make decisions so that others are subjects. Sanyika Shakur, also known as Monster Kody Scott, demonstrated moral agency as a former gang member who now, as a black nationalist, crusades against the causes of violent youth gangs.[37] Highly respected as a combat soldier with the Los Angeles gang the Crips, Kody earned the moniker "Monster" because he stomped into unconsciousness and permanently disfigured a man whom he and gang members were robbing. The police called the perpetrator a "monster," and his fellow gang members sanctioned the name; thus, Kody preferred "Monster" to his birth name.[38] After years of violent gang activity and several periods of incarceration, Kody experienced a complete political and personal transformation and officially renamed himself "Sanyika Shakur." He was transformed from being the violent gang member who was initiated into the gang at the age of eleven by shooting at rival gang members.[39] Now, his commitments are to his wife and family and the community where he grew up. His spiritual transformation compelled him to work against the institutional causes of gangsterism.[40] The ultimate transformation of Sanyika Shakur led him not only to make decisions that made others subjects, but also to confront institutional injustices, which effects the economic, political, and social well-being of other people. Thus, Sayika Shakur acts as a moral agent for the people of his community.

The challenge for the African American Christian church is to fashion male teenagers into moral agents, not only those in our congregations, but also those whom William Julius Wilson calls the "truly disadvantaged," as well as young black males who are labeled as superpredators.

Our Black Sons
Confronting Racial Profiling

One way of confronting the injustice of racial profiling is the socialization of black boys in the belief that they can be moral agents against racial profiling. From a broader perspective this means the socialization of our black sons to seek personal and public justice as an aspect of their spirituality, while practicing the spiritual disciplines of community activism and political activity. Such youth are nurtured in churches that espouse the spiritual tradition of social justice, argues Robert Franklin.[41]

Related to the fostering of moral agency in black male teenagers is a way of confronting injustice. In earlier research I sought to discover the presence and nature of the value of confronting oppressive authority in the lives of high school youth. Confronting oppressive authority means that the youth finds it necessary to respond in some manner to perceived injustice or unfairness during a conflict that they experience with an authority figure. A young person experiences a personal violation imposed by someone in authority and deems it necessary to respond in some manner. The analysis of this research resulted in four distinct patterns or typologies of confrontation. First, there is *instantaneous impulsivity*, which reflects an involuntary response to the oppressive experience. This knee-jerk response occurs during the moment of unfairness. Usually, it has a counterproductive effect on the situation. Second, *contextual praxis* addresses the cyclical, systematic movement of reflection, discourse, and response based on the presenting situation, and consists of the oppressive experience, the recognition of that act of oppression, reflection on the act, and the response. Third, *provisional forbearance* involves patient waiting until the crucial time to respond appropriately; then the oppressed person moves to end the oppressive situation. Forbearance implies a long-term endurance of dehumanization as an exercised mode of survival. Peter Paris offers the notion of this kind of forbearance, but with certain conditions determined by the oppressed.[42] Fourth, *dialectical avoidance* posits the choice of passivity as action. To choose to do nothing in itself presents an action response to oppression. This is the decision not to address the injustice. Just a fraction over 66 percent of the black male teenagers demonstrated the contextual praxis typology. The other three typologies were evenly distributed, with just over 11 percent for each typology.

The typologies of contextual praxis and provisional forbearance sug-gest healthy ways for black male teenagers to confront racial profiling. Mitch, whose life story and experiences of racial profiling we saw earlier in this chapter, demonstrated a strong proclivity for contextual praxis. Throughout his life story, Mitch showed evidence of cyclical reflection, discussion, and response to various situations where he felt that he had been treated unjustly. However, his response lacked concern for the sys-temic nature of racial profiling. Jason, on the other hand, showed a strong affinity for provisional forbearance, demonstrating a long and patient waiting period after the injustice that he experienced, and then moving to address the situation much in the manner of the contex-tual praxis typology. Emphasis is placed on forbearance, whereby Jason endures humiliation for survival purposes until he can address the injus-tice and, hopefully, effect change. These two typologies for confronting injustice are interrelated. Sometimes, a black boy singled out by the police should quickly reflect on the situation at hand, weighing each fact in the situation. At the same time, that boy should engage in noncombative discussion with the police while sorting out the facts of the situation, and then ultimately respond in a manner that effectively addresses the racial profiling. On other occasions, black boys should exercise forbearance in order to survive, and then later, from a location of safety, confront the political institution that condones racial profiling.

Indeed, these typologies are meaning-making processes, aspects of epistemology, as well as aspects of spirituality. In some instances, black boys are socialized to expect the police to seek them out and "pick on them." Some are also socialized to respond in ways such that they will survive these racist incidents. Although these typologies require further study, I believe that they offer possibilities for socializing our sons in ways of confronting injustice that are compatible with those congregations that espouse the spiritual tradition of social justice.

Notes

1. Steve Cooper, "A Closer Look at Racial Profiling," *The Quill* 89, no. 6 (July 2001): 55; online at *www.facsnet.org/tools/nbgs/p_thru_%20z/pq/profile.php3*.

2. Ibid.

3. Ibid.

4. Christopher Cooper, "Driving Scared," *New Jersey Law Journal* 165, no. 7 (August 13, 2001): S-9.

5. Ibid.

6. Cooper, "A Closer Look at Racial Profiling," 58.

7. Ibid.

8. Robert M. Franklin, *Another Day's Journey: Black Churches Confronting the American Crisis* (Minneapolis: Fortress Press, 1997), 84.

9. Alvin F. Poussaint and Amy Alexander, *Lay My Burden Down: Unraveling Suicide and the Mental Health Crisis among African-Americans* (Boston: Beacon Press, 2000), 59.

10. Cooper, "A Closer Look at Racial Profiling," 57.

11. Jawanza Kunjufu, *Countering the Conspiracy to Destroy Black Boys,* vols. 1–2 (Chicago: Afro-Am Publishing, 1985), 1:1.

12. Ibid., 1:7, 24, 16–17.

13. Ibid., 1:18.

14. Ibid., 1:27.

15. Ibid., 1:29.

16. Ibid., 1:31.

17. Ibid., 2:1–9.

18. Ibid., 2:19.

19. Ibid., 2:19–20.

20. Ibid., 2:44–45.

21. Ibid., 1:11.

22. Ibid., 1:27.

23. Ibid., 1:21.

24. Franklin, *Another Day's Journey,* 1–28.

25. Ibid., 83.

26. Ibid., 28.

27. Ibid., 85.

28. Ibid., 86–88.

29. Ibid., 89, 92.

30. Ibid., 94.

31. Ibid., 95–96.

32. Ibid., 96–99.

33. Ibid., 85.

34. Ibid., 98.

35. Ibid., 36.

36. Peter Paris, *The Social Teaching of the Black Churches* (Minneapolis: Fortress Press, 1985), 60.

37. See Sanyika Shakur, *Monster: The Autobiography of an L.A. Gang Member* (New York: Atlantic Monthly Press, 1993).

38. Ibid., 13–15.

39. Ibid., 8–13.

40. Ibid., 352–77.

41. Franklin, *Another Day's Journey,* 41–43.

42. Peter Paris, *The Spirituality of African Peoples: The Search for a Common Moral* (Minneapolis: Fortress Press, 1995), 141–42.

CHAPTER SIX

"I SNAPPED, MAN"

Teenage Rage

During July of 1999, I attended a workshop for teenaged girls and women who were preparing to engage other girls from a public housing complex in conversation about issues related to self-esteem. One of the adult women in the group, a high school science teacher, raised a concern about the potentially violent behavior of some black adolescents toward each other at school. The teacher emphasized how respect was a primary issue for black teens.[1] Disrespect, or "dissing," among teenagers could lead to violent consequences. Disrespect results in eye-to-eye contact, on the one hand, and violent name calling, on the other. Among those attending was a bright, seventeen-year-old young woman who was asked to respond to the teacher's comments. She took a deep breath, paused, and then passionately responded.

The essence of her statement was this: A lot of black teens are just angry. There is so much complication and pain in their lives that they are angry. They are helpless to address things that give them pain, so they carry all the anger inside. It comes out in a variety of ways. Sometimes, gestures such as neck swiveling and finger snapping express this anger. At other times, anger is expressed in playing the dozens or signifying. At worst, it results in fighting or gun violence. All are expressions of the rage they feel deep within.

After this young female prophet had lifted her voice, a somber silence fell over all attending. These prophetic words frame questions regarding the influence of rage on black adolescent spirituality and the challenge for the church. In this chapter I share reflections on rage in African American adolescents across the socioeconomic spectrum and the effects of rage on black youth's spirituality. I propose the idea of *holy indignation* as an aspect of African American adolescent spirituality. Holy indignation is the freedom to express anger against injustice in the sacred space of the Christian church and also in the public square of North American society.

I begin with vignettes from the life stories of two teenagers whom I interviewed in the Chicago area, André and Allie.

André

Seventeen-year-old André is a senior at Evanston Township High School. When he was two years old, his mother, father, and brother lived on the west side of Chicago with his grandmother. He said,

> We lived with at least eleven of us in one apartment with three rooms.... Then we moved from there to the north side of Chicago. That was a little bit better, that neighborhood. Then we moved to Evanston...to a house. The neighborhood was nice. Wasn't anybody standing out on the corner, you know.

André lived most of his early years in Chicago, and moved with his mother and older brother to Evanston during his high school years. He sincerely adores his mother for her strength and dependability, for keeping him safe and moving forward from hard times to better times. André said,

> She's just put up with a lot of stuff, really, from my father and from us. And she's just a strong black woman.... You will never see her break down.... She will never let anything happen to us. She's brought us a long way.

Also, André holds his brother in high esteem for his ability to persevere and excel academically in spite of family problems. André's father struggles with alcoholism, which sometimes causes violent conflicts within the family, especially between his mother and father. "The lowest point in my life was dealing with that.... I don't know if I should love him or hate him." The family conflict took a great toll on André's grades during elementary and junior high school. However, André's father moved away while they were living on the north side of Chicago.

His congregation also has been pivotal in bringing happiness and fulfillment to André's life. He and his family attend a Pentecostal church on the south side of Chicago. He has vivid memories of participating in the children's Christmas pageant, how the congregation adored the kids dressed up in costumes, singing and reciting memorized Scriptures and speeches. When he was in elementary school, Sundays were very long. He got up early, missing cartoons, and took the long train and bus ride to 115th Street. Sunday School and worship followed fellowship dinner, and perhaps an evening service as well. The most memorable moment for André was his first conversation with his pastor, "in her office," he gleefully explained. He was about seven years old at that time and living on the north side. This is how André described that experience:

> She had called me in...to see her —you know, one on one. It was just crazy. Every Sunday, we looked at her like somebody, godly, somebody that you couldn't talk loud around. You had to whisper. You couldn't run past her; you had to walk, and hold your head down in submission. I mean, you couldn't say a bad word, or any that could be thought of as a bad word, call somebody stupid.... And to have her call me and sit down and talk to me —you know, she could see that I was hurting....It was hard to handle, being young...talking to her. She seemed just like everybody else, but she just had a role in life, and I never met anybody who was like that, and that's what she was doing....She was talking to me about doing good and to excel....She was just saying, like, things that were affecting me personally. She could see that I was dealing with a lot of things that I couldn't deal with, being young, and that I really needed to let it out —you know, to let it out into the church, to let the church help me deal with it. And she was telling me a lot of stuff that really came to pass.

The relationship that André had with his pastor and other children and adults motivated him to call his congregation "family." They shared disappointments, struggles. They collectively experienced displacement when the church's building burned. Biological and church family are pivotal in André's maturity and ability to be introspective.

André admits that his anger is particularly noticeable with persons in authority who treat him unfairly. He especially noted anger with his schoolteachers. He said, "Throughout my academic career I've not been able to deal with the authority of teachers, telling me...I mean, it's a certain way you can tell somebody, man, you want them to do something." He recalled his eighth-grade teacher who said, " 'The way you are acting, you will never be anything but a garbage man or a waiter.' I could not deal with that. That was hard, being told you'll never be anything. . . . That's the hardest thing for me ever to hear. Oh, I snapped, man. I was young, and I went off and told her what she could do. I cursed her kinda good. I was kicked out of school for a week. I have learned now." He described his recent response after four years. André said,

> I recently visited her last semester. I showed her my report card. She was trying to be all nice, saying, "Oh, I'm proud of you, Mr. Thomas." . . . I was nice. I'm not going to be mean. I was like, "How are you doing Ms. So-and-so?" I'm not going to say her name. "You remember me? I was in your class." She was, like, "Yeah, you have grown." And I was, like, "Yeah. . . . You remember that day, remember all the problems we used to have when I was younger? I've changed. I'm doing really well in school now. I'd like you to look at my report card." She looked at it. . . . She said she was proud of me — this and that. I was, like, just to show you were wrong . . . that's what I said to myself. I mean, I just look back; I was just proud of myself. I changed so much from just coming to Evanston. . . . If I was back in Chicago, how would I be?

André admits that when he and his family lived on the west side of Chicago, he hung around with older boys who were gang members. "I was like their little brother, like a little kid who . . . tags along. . . . I saw the older guys fighting and all that stuff." When his family moved to the north side of Chicago, André became an affiliate with the neighborhood gang for protection rather than being initiated as a full member.

During tenth grade, when André's low grades threatened his position on the football team, he evaluated aspects of his life and devised a plan for study and improving his grades and for fun times with his friends. This plan pulled up his grades and moved him into the varsity football league. His accomplishments brought him public fame. André said that his success helped him to forgive "everything, everybody I fought with, everybody I didn't like, everybody that didn't like me — it didn't matter." In fact, André said that if he were to write his autobiography, the chapters would be on family, survival, and forgiveness. The theme of forgiveness weaves together the *kente* cloth of André's life. "Being able to forgive the people that hurt me" is how André describes this third chapter of his life.

Allie

Like André, Allie deeply values her family. This seventeen-year-old high school senior lives with her mother, brother, and sister in Evanston. She frequently spends weekends with her paternal grandparents on the south side of Chicago. Allie's father is very much a part of her life even though he does not live in the household with her. She is his only child, and she boasts of how her father and his parents have spoiled her. Allie calls some of her maternal and fraternal cousins "my best friends." These friends and cousins, along with her grandparents, mother (who took time off from work), siblings, and boyfriend, were with her at her sixteenth birthday parties, one in Evanston and one on the south side of Chicago. They prepared Allie's favorite dishes, including "Southern-fried chicken, buttermilk biscuits, . . . collard greens and mustard greens, . . . and corn bread." Allie said, "And then my mother had gotten this big chocolate cake, because I love chocolate." The big birthday meal lasted most of the day. That evening, her paternal grandmother cooked "pork chops . . . and greens. . . . And everybody came over. It was fun. I really enjoyed it. I didn't get a whole lot of presents, but just the fact that everybody was together just for that little event — that was fun," said Allie.

Allie is endeared to her family, immediate and extended, and celebrates the good times they have shared. However, she is realistic about pain she has experienced in her family — "the people I've loved and I've lost" is how she describes it. Memories of her nephew, whom she considered to be her "best friend," spins Allie into a valley of grief and brings tears to her eyes. This was a nephew by marriage, just two years older than Allie, who tragically died in a train accident. She said, "I mean, [he] was my truly best friend. I could tell him anything. And [*pauses while crying*] he died when I was twelve, and that's when I couldn't do nothing. I couldn't go to school. I wouldn't go to church. I was mad at God. I was mad at the world. And it's still hard for me to talk about it. And he would have been twenty this year."

Allie considers Thanksgiving to be a religious holiday because members of her family are together. She struggles in choosing the family with which she will spend Thanksgiving. She comments, "They're always like playing a tug of war with me, but it's still special because I have a lot of things to be thankful for, because I know that it's a lot of love that we have."

Allie is a member of a Baptist church in Evanston where her maternal grandmother and some of her other grandchildren attend. A very exciting time for Allie was her participation in the "Black History Month" program organized by a cousin who is a deacon at their church. He had Allie write poems and select one to recite during the program. Allie said, "That was, like, the highest point of my life in church. . . . I enjoyed it. That was fun. . . . I got to say it in front of, like, my preacher. . . . At that time he meant a lot to me because when my [maternal] granddad died, he was there for me. . . . So he stepped in. He was like my granddad."

Allie's poem was about black women and based on Toni Morrison's book *The Bluest Eye*. Allie was concerned that her grandmother would say that the poem was inappropriate for church, but Allie's fear was unwarranted. Her grandmother was pleased.

The same pastor whom Allie wanted so much to please with her original poem died a year after the Black History Month program. This was by far the saddest experience for Allie and for the youth and adults in her congregation. "Because he had been my preacher all my life," said Allie. She described the occasion of his funeral as being filled with adults wailing in anguish, so much so that the youth stepped in to console the pastor's widow and other adults in the congregation.

Joy and sorrow in her biological family and church family is a dominant theme in Allie's life story. However, even amid the times of grief, Allie has looked to the strength of her grandmothers and her mother as her model for perseverance.

Allie talked about her values in life, which include education, money, and, more importantly, her family. She said, "Family is very important to me. I don't allow anyone to come in and hurt my family." When I asked for her to give me an example, she replied,

It was this incident at school, and my mom had to go up there because I was having a problem with a teacher. And she raised her voice at my mom. And I [*pauses*] I admit I was wrong for coming at the teacher the way I did, so my mom had to take me out of the room because I was gonna hit her, . . . because I felt you don't disrespect somebody if they're trying to respect you. The teacher raised her voice at my mom, and she was talking to [my mom] like she was a little girl or something. So, man! Family is, like, everything to me, everything.

When Allie was asked about the extent to which she would stand on behalf of her family, she responded emphatically that she would sacrifice her life for family if necessary.

Another example of how Allie expresses her rage in the presence of unjust acts by persons in authority is recalled in an incident of racial profiling involving her father when he was pulled over while traveling home to the south side of Chicago. Allie commented,

> He has a Volvo. He has money. He's a pharmacist. He's going to school, like, forever! And the police officers pulled him over, and I was in the car. He told me to sit in the car, and I watched them, like, do him like that. The police officers told him to spread his arms out and all this, to search him. . . . After he had searched him and the car, the cop says, "I'm sorry, but we thought that you were a drug dealer. You fit the description of a drug dealer." And I couldn't say anything at that time, because I was young.

Allie was ten years old at this time, experiencing rage at the racial profiling in her father's encounter with the police. Six years later, Allie and her boyfriend were pulled over by the police. She admits that they were speeding, but emphasizes that there was no point in the police putting her friend through such a harsh ordeal. Allie spoke up to the police on this occasion. She asked the police questions and wrote down the badge number of the officer. She said,

> That's how you can make a change. You have to think. Because my boyfriend . . . was, like, "I'm gonna get him." . . . You know we were both angry because we knew he was wrong. And the police officer wasn't white. He was black, and he was doing him like that. That doesn't make any sense. . . . That's how you deal with injustice. You have to talk about it. You can't fight violence with violence all the time. You can't do that, because everybody ends up hurt.

These snapshots of André's and Allie's life stories illustrate acts of injustice that they have experienced that made them angry. It also illustrates their way of coping. They have shared their deep feelings of being driven to rage, both expressed and held inside. Their rage resulted from being berated and belittled by teachers and harassed by the police. They sometimes found themselves helpless and unable to defend and protect self and family. They have known rage from being silenced. This is the type

of rage that the young lady in the opening of this chapter prophetically
addressed. How does one account for André's and Allie's rage, and for
the rage of so many African American adolescents? What is the connection between their rage and their spirituality? Answers to these questions
must begin with a historical look at the function and residual effects of
rage in the African American community.

Black Rage

The rage that André and Allie felt is not a new topic of concern. Sociologists and psychologists have written about the rage found among African
Americans. The classic book *Black Rage,* by psychiatrists William H. Grier
and Price M. Cobbs, addresses the root causes of rage in black adults.
First published in 1968, and now in its fourth printing, this book examines the full range of black life, revealing the desperation, conflicts, and
anger of blacks in America.[2] Grier and Cobbs argue that the insidious and
residual effects of the heritage of slavery, and the psychic stresses engendered by discrimination, are central to black rage.[3] The rage caused by
white oppression of blacks has psychological consequences. Grier and
Cobbs argue that "the culture that was born in the experience of bondage
has been passed from generation to generation" among African Americans. The brutality of white oppression from the beginning of slavery
to the present "is narrowed, focused, and refined to shine into a black
child's eyes when first she views her world. All that has ever happened
to black men and women she sees in the victims closest to her, her parents." "Depression and grief are hatred turned on the self. It is instructive
to pursue the relevance of this truth to the condition of black Americans."[4] This is the evidence of black rage. The authors acknowledge the
tremendous ability of blacks to survive, but recognize that it has taken a
psychological toll on black people. I contend that although black people
have shown a genius for surviving under the most deadly circumstances,
this skill often is absent in twenty-first-century black youth.

Grier and Cobbs acknowledge the research and abundance of materials written by psychiatrists and psychologists subsequent to the first
edition of their book. They write, "It is exciting to witness the scholarship
now focused on the mental health of blacks, the factors affecting it, and
the remedies as well."[5] In the 1992 edition they express appreciation for

those who show "the continued interest in issues of race, child development, society, and of oppression and its consequences for the oppressor and the oppressed."[6] Examples of subsequent research and publication include specialized research on black adolescents and reach beyond the discipline of psychology to sociology, religious studies, and journalism.

The 1993 book *The Rage of a Privileged Class,* by Ellis Cose, is an examination of rage from the perspective of a journalist writing about the problem of race in North American society. Cose examines the anger of middle-class black Americans who have been successful professionally but have been rejected by middle-class white America. Cose calls this "the problem of the broken covenant," of the pact ensuring that with hard work, a good education, and playing by the rules of society, a black professional will be allowed to advance and achieve to the extent of her or his ability.[7] The laments of those who "had every accoutrement of success" were:

> I have done everything I was supposed to do. I have stayed out of trouble with the law, gone to the right schools, and worked myself nearly to death. What more do they want? Why in God's name won't they accept me as a full human being? Why am I pigeonholed in a "black job"? Why am I constantly treated as if I were a drug addict, a thief, or a thug? Why am I still not allowed to aspire to the same things every white person in America takes as a birthright? Why, when I most want to be seen, am I suddenly rendered invisible?[8]

Cose explores the meaning of these questions and attempts to provide answers. Highlighting Cecil Williams, former pastor of Glide Memorial United Methodist Church in San Francisco, Cose discusses Williams's experiences of coping with racism during his childhood in San Angelo, Texas. At the age of ten, Williams experienced a nervous breakdown following the death of his grandfather and witnessing the barring of his body's burial from the white area of the cemetery. Williams was crippled by a loss of faith that resulted in insanity.[9] The ghost of those experiences continued to crop up in Williams's life even after his success in leading a multiracial church committed to justice. Even as pastor, Williams felt that his parishioners respected him only as long as he could make things work. When things went wrong, some parishioners would reject him. Williams shared one such event with Cose:

[Williams] still feels that he can never fully let his racial guard down; for ghosts from the graveyard in San Angelo, Texas, continue to reappear. "Every once in a while," he said, "when one of my white AIDS patients dies, they go to some other place . . . and they have the memorial." Just the other day, the mother of one such parishioner had made plans to have her son memorialized by a white pastor. That decision, it was clear, had caused Williams pain; and made him feel used: "As long as I can be of service to you, and make things work for you, then you're here. But when it's over, then you go to some other place."

Williams considered the mother's deed "an act of racism." He smiled, adding, "those things crop up." Even if he personally did not experience prejudice, "I would still know there was a lot of work to be done." He never allowed himself to assume that "I got it made with white folks," because "when the chips are down . . . they're not going to come to me, more than likely."[10]

This demonstrates how Williams copes with racism and with the rage it generates.

After sharing Williams's story, Cose discusses the "twelve demons" with which blacks spend time coping:[11]

1. *Inability to fit in.* Blacks cope with marginalization in the workplace when white executives feel that blacks would be out of place in certain positions.

2. *Exclusion from the club.* Blacks cope with the fact that even if a black fits in, that does not guarantee acceptance.

3. *Low expectations.* Blacks cope with believing that success is not within their grasp. Such hopelessness results in anger.

4. *Shattered hopes.* Blacks cope with rage resulting from destroyed dreams in the workplace.

5. *Faint praise.* Blacks cope with attitudes of whites that communicate that they are among the gifted few African Americans.

6. *Presumption of failure.* Black professionals cope with the assumption that failure at the highest corporate levels is reserved for whites.

7. *Coping with fatigue.* Becoming exhausted from struggles to be accepted and respected for their abilities regardless of their race,

blacks drop out of their professions. They lose desire to achieve because of the energy needed for coping.

8. *Pigeonholing.* Blacks cope with placements in executive positions where the only relevant expertise is concern for blacks and other minorities.

9. *Identity troubles.* Blacks cope with the consequence that confronting racism may be costly, so much so that they jettison their racial identity.

10. *Self-censorship and silence.* Blacks cope with finding their voices stilled when sensitive issues of race surface.

11. *Mendacity.* Blacks cope with the falsification of racial situations within the corporate world, such as deceptions about companies being color-blind and an unwillingness to admit racial bias.

12. *Guilt by association.* Blacks cope with mistaken identity that results from whites who refuse to distinguish one black person from another.

Cose's list of causes for rage in light of coping with racism among blacks is not exclusive for blacks; it is relevant to the experiences of other minorities.

Cose's discussion of rage among middle-class blacks then shifts to concern for young people. He refers back to chapter 1, where he discusses the rage of Ulric Haynes, former ambassador to Algeria under President Carter's administration. Haynes discusses his hopelessness of racial parity ever arriving in his lifetime, nor that of his children or his grandchildren. His laments are expressed in rage. Cose quotes Haynes as saying, "I'm angry for the deception that this has perpetrated on my children and grandchildren." Though his children have traveled the world and received an elite education, Haynes notes, they "in a very real sense are not the children of privilege. They are dysfunctional, because I didn't prepare them, in all the years we lived overseas, to deal with the climate of racism they are encountering right now."[12] Black middle-class parents experience rage that their children are not benefiting from the privileges for which they have worked. Likewise, these children are unprepared for the racial situations they experience when they leave the cocoon that protects young middle-class blacks from racism. I have heard anecdotal accounts of middle-class youth who attend Southern Methodist University facing the harsh realities of racism in the communities adjacent to the school. Racial profiling of black male students driving in adjacent neighborhoods is particularly frequent.

Cose concludes his book stating that the racial gap in U.S. society can be bridged only by first recognizing the issues of race that divide society and cause rage in those who experience racism.

Both books, *Black Rage* and *The Rage of the Privileged Class,* give insight into the anger expressed by African American adults. Similarly, the anthology *Black Adolescents,* edited by Reginald L. Jones and published in 1989, presents a variety of problems facing black adolescents in urban and rural settings. The majority of the eight chapters "share perspectives that emphasize how race, socioeconomic status, and environmental forces shape this critical period in the life of Black adolescents."[13] Historical snapshots of rage in the life of African Americans suggest the far-reaching effects of anger on African Americans.

Black Adolescent Rage and Class

African American adolescent rage can also be discussed in terms of issues of class. The rage of black underclass, working poor rural and inner-city black teens is different from that of middle- and upper-class black teens in the suburbs. The stresses that poor, inner-city black teens experience, such as substandard housing and neighborhoods, "multiple marginalities and social control, as well as lack of economic opportunities,"[14] are different from the stresses felt by middle- and upper-class black teens. The stresses on the latter group include pressure to achieve academically and socially in the white-dominated milieu of their schools and suburban neighborhoods. The Center for Disease Control (CDC) and psychologist Carl Bell have discussed the problem of suicide among middle-class black youth. Consider a quotation that illustrates hopelessness and internalized rage among middle- and upper-class black teens.

> In addition to factors such as drugs and the breakdown of the family, the CDC suggested African-Americans in upwardly mobile families are dealing with more stress and may adopt the coping behaviors of the larger society, in which suicide may be more commonly used to deal with hopelessness and depression. Carl Bell, an African-American mental health expert who works with black

youngsters in Chicago, points out that middle-class blacks feel alienated at a young age. "You don't belong in any world," he said. "You don't belong in the white middle-class and you don't belong among poor blacks. There is an alienation that occurs."[15]

Black adolescent rage, particularly among inner-city youth, can manifest itself in forms of violence. James Garbarino's *Lost Boys: Why Our Sons Turn Violent and How We Can Save Them* responds to the question of the origin of violence particularly among inner-city youth regardless of ethnicity. His review of the work of psychologist Robert Zagar indicates seven primary factors that put boys at risk to commit murder. Although Garbarino focuses on violence among boys, not girls, his list of reasons for violent boys is instructive. Here are the seven factors that Garbarino discusses:

1. *Child abuse.* Research indicates that the rate of child abuse of children with a history of maltreatment rose from 14 per 100,000 to 23 per 100,000 during the period 1986–93. Those children at risk for maltreatment nearly doubled as well.

2. *Gangs.* Statistics from the federal government report that more and more communities are experiencing the problem of youth gangs. These gangs are widespread in inner-city communities.

3. *Substance abuse.* "Hard drugs have spread throughout the United States; virtually every community in the country has a drug subculture."[16] The CDC reports that 9 percent of all high-school-aged males have used cocaine. More than 50 percent of adolescent boys reported using marijuana. In 1976, the use of marijuana was on the decline; since 1994, research indicates, the use of marijuana has been increasing. In addition to drug abuse is the problem of heavy alcohol use among adolescents.

4. *Weapons.* A 1997 CDC survey reveals that 28 percent of the adolescent boys carried a weapon —a gun, knife, or club —in the previous month, with 13 percent carrying a weapon to school in the previous month.

5. *Arrests.* Arrests of youth under age eighteen are up 50 percent from 1980 to 1994 for serious offenses.

6. *Neurological problems.* There has been a significant increase among children with conditions such as Attention Deficit Disorder (ADD), which results in behavioral problems. More and more kids are living with neurological difficulties, as a result of their immaturity, that can impair the processes of thinking and feeling.

7. *Difficulties at school.* Data shows that for any thirty-day period, about one in three high school kids report having skipped school at least one day. There is a correlation between the household constellation and the likelihood of a kid skipping school. Kids from a mother-only household tend to skip class more than kids from two-parent households. "According to the 1997 CDC survey, twenty percent of all high-school-age boys reported that they were in a physical fight on school property in the past year."[17] Uncontrolled rage results in some of the destructive behaviors described above. Rage that is translated into resistance can be illustrated through hip-hop and its primary musical form, rap.

The Rage of Hip-Hop Culture

Hip-hop culture provides examples of rage born in the urban context and continues to communicate expressions of rage not only among inner-city youth, but also among youth across the ethnic and socioeconomic strata. "Hip hop culture first emerges as a cultural and creative response to the matrix of industrial decline, social isolation, and political decay endemic to New York City's Bronx section."[18] Hip-hop culture includes not only various types of rap music, but also movies, videos, styles of dress, and a particular language. Additionally, hip-hop culture created its own dance form as early as 1973, known as "break dancing," and graffiti as a visual artistic expression, which emerged as early as 1971. Hip-hop culture indicates cultural resistance and a postmodern initiative to circumvent the powerlessness that urban youth experience under the dominant society.[19] Tricia Rose's 1994 book *Black Noise: Rap Music and Black Culture in Contemporary America* offers a comprehensive examination of "complex and contradictory relationships between forces of racial and sexual domination, black cultural priorities, and popular resistance in contemporary rap music."[20] Anthony Pinn and Michael Eric Dyson are two theologians who have written extensively about hip-hop culture, particularly rap music, articulating its influence on the African American community and greater U.S. society.

I want to focus briefly on rage in hip-hop culture's movies, graffiti, and rap music. First, let us examine rage in film. Two of the earliest movies depicting adolescent rage in urban life are *Do the Right Thing* and *Boyz N the Hood*. Spike Lee's 1989 film *Do the Right Thing* depicts the fomenting rage of a young pizza delivery man, Mookie, played by Lee. Rap music provides the beat for mounting rage among Mookie and a host of others in his Brooklyn neighborhood, including Sal (Danny Aiello), an Italian-American and the owner of Sal's Famous Pizzeria, and Pino (John Turturro), Sal's angry young bigoted son. The pulsating sounds of rap music foreshadow the rage that explodes into violence and the eventual death of Radio Raheem (Bill Nunn), who carries a large "boom box." *Do the Right Thing is* an exceptional illustration of hip hop culture's earlier films depicting adolescent rage.

Boyz N the Hood, the 1991 film directed by John Singleton, portrays the rage of gang life in south-central Los Angeles. Singleton captures the full array of urban life, including the pervasiveness of the drug problem, police harassment, poverty, the high incidence of death among black youth, and the effects of such social stresses on family life. Gangsta rap artist Ice Cube gained critical acclaim for his portrayal of the character Dough Boy in *Boyz N the Hood*. Ice Cube was among a group of artists known as Niggaz With Attitude (N.W.A.), which gave birth to gangsta rap. It is a rap music form that started in the Compton and Watts areas of Los Angeles during the 1980s. This music is characterized by misogynistic and violent language, "raw aggression and reckless lifestyle." Sometimes, gangsta rap offers a critique of society, "demonstrating the destruction done to humans by market-driven goals."[21] Gangsta rap music is heard in *Boyz N the Hood,* and Ice Cube, one of its leading characters, lives out the rage caused by his social milieu, and dies from the rage generated from drive-by shootings by violent gangs.

The music of hip-hop culture —rap music —launched its place in popular culture during the early 1970s. Anthony Pinn categorizes rap music as "status" rap, "gansta" (also spelled "gangsta") rap, and "progressive" rap. Status rap communicates concerns about status and social prowess. Gangsta rap represents the double concern for arriving at the American dream via its consumerism while offering a critique of dehumanizing practices in U.S. society. Progressive rap seeks to transform systems of injustice by transforming the perspective of their victims.[22] Progressive rap music demonstrates the clear prophetic voice reflecting the rage caused by the dehumanizing injustices that African Americans experience. Two progressive rap songs illustrate my point. "Don't push me, 'cause I'm close to the edge. I'm tryin' not to lose my head. It's like a jungle sometimes, it makes me wonder how I keep from going under." These lyrics are the refrain from the hip-hop song *The Message* by Grand Master Flash. He describes the rage he feels from the chaos of urban life. Grand Master Flash speaks his rage in the earshot of the public square, making known his discontent and dismay with disparaging situations of the urban milieu. Public Enemy, the moniker of "hip-hop's preeminent voice of prophetic rage"[23] during the late 1980s, has confronted white supremacy, black bourgeoisie conservatives, and the misogyny of gangsta rap music. These rap-music artists are a small sampling of those who voice the rage of young people living in the inner city.

The visual art expression of rage from hip-hop culture also comes through graffiti artists. These artists spray-paint murals and "tags" (name tags) on trains, trucks, and playgrounds, claiming territories and inscribing their otherwise contained identities on public property. Crews ordinarily create graffiti work using the urban transit system as their canvas and aided by the technology of spray paint. Crews are a local source of identity, group affiliation, and support system. Tagging, it appears, did not originate with black and Hispanic inner-city youth, but with a Greek teenager named Demetrius from the Washington Heights section of Manhattan, New York.[24] Demetrius, known as Taki 183 on subway cars and stations, buildings, and billboards, started the graffiti movement adopted by teenagers. The *New York Times* tracked Taki 183 down and interviewed him in 1971.

By the mid-1970s, graffiti became more complex, as it developed "elaborate individual styles, themes, formats, and techniques, most of which were designed to increase visibility, individual identity, and status. Themes in the larger works include hip hop slang, characterizations of b-boys, rap lyrics, and hip hop fashion."[25] Train facades are important to graffiti murals, lending visual impact through the movement of the train. Also, a considerable amount of risk is involved with graffiti murals in dangerous train yards, as well as the purchase of outlawed supplies such as spray paints and permanent markers. Graffiti artists, both male and female, usually work alongside each other in train yards and atop public buildings. Their work is often motivated by social criticism.[26]

Since the late 1970s, tagging has become a form of juvenile delinquency in New York City and other major cities. Eventually, graffiti artists were sought after for criminal prosecution, as allowed by antigraffiti public policy, and millions of dollars were provided to prevent graffiti artists.[27] Graffiti artists give voice and image to the rage of urban youth. They risk life and limb to resist the silencing that U.S. society imposes upon them through their images that tower over the posh areas of financial districts and travel on commuter trains to gated suburban neighborhoods.

Hip-hop culture expresses the rage of inner-city black youth as well as urban youth from other ethnic communities. This rage is generated by racial and social domination imposed upon those within the urban context. The powerlessness that black teens feel is expressed in hip-hop culture through movies, videos, rap music, and graffiti art. There is little evidence that the church has functioned to help black youth express their rage in a "sacred space"[28] in relation to the holy in addition to the public area. I want to explore this idea through the concept of *holy indignation* as a significant contribution to emancipatory hope.

Holy Indignation

How can youth claim the anger that they experience from being treated unjustly as good anger? How is anger holy? What might the church and community consider that will empower black youth to channel their rage in such a way that they experience spiritual edification and political efficacy? How can youth move beyond merely acquiring skills of conflict management to sculpturing a spirituality that emulates the indignation of God? I offer the idea of holy indignation in light of these questions. Holy indignation is best understood through a definition of indignation, the root word in this concept. Indignation is anger aroused by something unjust within a human relationship. Treated as synonymous with rage, wrath, and anger, indignation expresses a violated connection between human beings that yearns to be mended. Indignation is human wrath demonstrated in words or deeds against forces that hinder human thriving. To describe indignation as holy connotes the divine nature of human rage. To have holy indignation is to model God's emotion in the midst of injustice between God and God's people. Holy indignation emulates the holiness of God, whose wrath is shown when Israel fractures its connection with God through disobedience:

> The LORD said to Moses, "Go down at once! Your people, whom you brought up out of the land of Egypt, have acted perversely; they have been quick to turn aside from the way that I commanded them...." The LORD said to Moses, "I have seen this people, how stiff-necked they are. Now let me alone, so that my wrath may burn hot against them." (Exodus 32:7–10)

Throughout the Hebrew Bible, holy Yahweh expresses anger at wayward Israel, severing its relationship from God.

Many theologians have asked, "Can we speak consistently of God as both a God of love and a God of wrath?"[29] Some answer yes. This may suggest "that the anger of a loving God is the reaction of a God who cares, who chides us and derides us in order to bring us back to our senses."[30] Psalmists also have spoken of God's indignation in conjunction with God's justice and righteousness in times of trouble. Psalm 7 is a prayer for help from a person being encroached upon by enemies.[31] In verse 11, the psalmist declares, "God is a righteous judge, and a God who has indignation every day." God is a righteous judge whose anger moves God daily toward protecting the "upright in heart."[32] In Psalm 38:3, the psalmist is penitent, seeking healing from God rather than illness and pain. The psalmist says, "There is no soundness in my flesh because of your indignation; there is no health in my bones because of my sin." Psalm 69 is a petition for protection against the psalmist's enemies. Psalm 69:24 implores, "Pour out your indignation upon them, and let your burning anger overtake them." God's indignation on the psalmist's opponent is sought.

The prophet Jeremiah admonishes Israel regarding idolatry. At the end of prophesied words from God in Jeremiah 10:2–5, Jeremiah offers praises to God in verses 6–10. Verse 10 declares, "But the LORD is the true God; he is the living God and the everlasting King. At his wrath the earth quakes, and the nations cannot endure his indignation." In Jeremiah 15, Jeremiah offers a prophetic lament regarding his task as a prophet as well as his enemies. In Jeremiah 15:16–17, he invokes God to intervene on his behalf "as he protests his innocence and his devotion to his prophetic calling."[33] In Jeremiah 15:17, he asserts, "I did not sit in the company of merrymakers, nor did I rejoice; under the weight of your hand I sat alone, for you had filled me with indignation." Patrick Miller comments on this passage:

> Jeremiah advances his case for fidelity to his calling (v. 17). It has meant his isolation from those who were enjoying life, whether the false prophet of peace or the people. His harsh words of judgement, intended by the term "indignation," have made him unwelcome at the party! God has put him into this terrible spot. The "weight of your hand," or more simply, "your hand," alludes to the prophetic call or burden. He is under the claim, the authority of the Lord, and because of this is thrust into this position of isolation and loneliness.[34]

Jeremiah, the young prophet, claims the divine "indignation" from God that empowers him to speak on God's behalf, even when it is not popular. The prophet's message subverts the negative connotations about rage that are widely held today into a positive and divine emotion that can provide power for adolescent girls and boys.

Like the psalmists and Jeremiah, the eighth-century prophet Micah invokes indignation in Micah 7. Micah identifies with the poor and oppressed and acknowledges his call to prophesy on Yahweh's behalf. In Micah 7:9, he declares, "I must bear the indignation of the LORD, because I have sinned against him, until he takes my side and executes judgment for me. He will bring me out to the light; I shall see his vindication." Micah indicates that he must endure God's anger because of his sins.

Through these Scriptures I have tried to illustrate how the word "indignation" has been used in prayers of petition, in laments, and to describe God's passion toward wayward Israel. Similarly, New Testament texts do not teach us that anger is wrong, but that uncontrolled anger has potential for destruction. For example, Paul urges, "Be angry but do not sin; do not let the sun go down on your anger" (Ephesians 4:26).

In her essay "The Power of Anger in the Work of Love," Beverly Harrison, a professor of Christian social ethics, writes,

> Anger is not the opposite of love. It is better understood as a feeling-signal that *all is not well* in our relation to other persons or groups or

to the world around us. Anger is a *mode of connectedness* to others and it is always a *vivid form of caring.*[35]

Holy indignation is the freedom to express anger against injustice in the sacred space of the Christian church and also in the public square. It is the congregation's act of sanctification and sanction upon those youth who desire to transform systems of domination and oppressive power structures. As members of the household of faith, African American adolescents have the right to stand within the congregation, even in the midst of the sanctuary, and express their rage. The congregation of all ages has the responsibility to nurture adolescents' rage, to help teens hone this anger into a fine-tuned rational emotion that promotes wholeness and human flourishing for themselves, their families, and local and global communities.

Holy indignation is akin to righteous indignation in that it focuses on anger justified because of ethical concerns about wrongful acts. The church needs to foster holy indignation because Scripture validates the positive aspect of holy indignation. Adults in ministry with black youth model holy indignation in the sacred space of the congregation, as well as affirming the positive nature of rage.

Notes

1. Elsewhere I have written about the issues of respect and honor among youth. See Evelyn L. Parker, "Hungry for Honor: Children in Violent Youth Gangs," *Interpretation* 55, no. 2 (April 2001): 148–60.

2. William H. Grier and Price M. Cobbs, *Black Rage* (San Francisco: Basic Books/HarperCollins, 1992), back cover.

3. Ibid.

4. Ibid., 207, 31, 208.

5. Ibid., xii.

6. Ibid., viii–ix.

7. Ellis Cose, *The Rage of a Privileged Class* (New York: HarperPerennial, 1995), 1.

8. Ibid.

9. Ibid., 53–54.

10. Ibid., 54.

11. Ibid., 56–68.

12. Ibid., 6.

13. Reginald Jones, *Black Adolescents* (Berkeley, Calif.: Cobb and Henry, 1989), xi.

14. Shirley Brice Heath and Milbrey W. McLaughlin, "Building Identities for Inner-City Youth," in *Identity and Inner-City Youth: Beyond Ethnicity and Gender,* ed. Shirley Brice Heath and Milbrey W. McLaughlin (New York: Teachers College Press, 1993), 9.

15. Evelyn L. Parker, "Theological Framework for Youth Ministry: Hope," in *Starting Right: Thinking Theologically about Youth Ministry,* ed. Kenda Creasy Dean, Chap Clark, and David Rahn (Grand Rapids: Zondervan, 2001), 267.

16. James Garbarino, *Lost Boys: Why Our Sons Turn Violent and How We Can Save Them* (New York: Free Press, 1999), 13.

17. Ibid., 15.

18. Anthony B. Pinn, *Why Lord? Suffering and Evil in Black Theology* (New York: Continuum, 1995), 122.

19. Ibid.

20. Tricia Rose, *Black Noise: Rap Music and Black Culture in Contemporary America* (Hanover, N.H.: University Press of New England, 1994), xiii.

21. Pinn, *Why Lord?* 124, 127.

22. Ibid., 125–34.

23. Michael Eric Dyson, *Between God and Gangsta Rap* (New York: Oxford University Press, 1996), 167.

24. Rose, *Black Noise,* 22, 34, 41–42.

25. Ibid., 42–44.

26. Ibid., 44.

27. Ibid., 44–45.

28. I borrow this term from Emilie Townes, who argues that discursive space can best approximate sacredness rather than safe space.

29. Alastair V. Campbell, "The Anger of a Loving God," *Modern Churchman* 25, no. 3 (1983): 2.

30. Ibid.

31. J. Clinton McCann, "The Book of Psalms," in *The New Interpreter's Bible,* vol. 4 (Nashville: Abingdon Press, 1996), 707.

32. Ibid., 708.

33. Patrick D. Miller, "The Book of Jeremiah," in *The New Interpreter's Bible,* vol. 6 (Nashville: Abingdon Press, 2001) 697.

34. Ibid., 698.

35. Beverly W. Harrison, "The Power of Anger in the Work of Love: Christian Ethics for Women and Other Strangers," in *Making the Connections,* ed. Carol S. Robb (Boston: Beacon Press), 4.

CHAPTER SEVEN

HOPING AGAINST HOPE?

"Hoping against hope, [Abraham] believed that he would become 'the father of many nations,' according to what was said, 'So numerous shall you descendants be.' ... being fully convinced that God was able to do what he had promised" (Romans 4:18, 21). In these verses from his letter to the church in Rome, Paul illustrates the nature of faith by recalling the experiences of Abraham and Sarah. Because of their old age, all logical reasoning would suggest that Abraham and Sarah would never have a child. But Paul suggests that Abraham demonstrated hope in God's promises that he would have descendants. Abraham's faith positioned him to believe that God would keep the promise of his fatherhood. The idea of emancipatory hope posits this type of faith in God. No matter how irrational or impossible something may seem, God's promises are true. Like Abraham, we are convinced that God is able to deliver on God's promises.

The idea of emancipatory hope means the expectation of the transformation of hegemonic relations and to act as God's agent bringing in God's vision of equality for humankind. The spirituality of one who possesses emancipatory hope receives the gift of the African and African American ancestors who lived an intricately woven life of divine and human activity against forms of domination. Emancipatory hope is an intricately woven life of both pious and political existence that focuses on critical consciousness and critical action so that racial, economic, social, and political domination is eradicated.

What is the nature of leadership among teenagers and adults necessary for fostering the emancipatory hope that is essential to African American adolescent spirituality? How can youth pastors, lay youth advisors, church school teachers for youth, and youth choir directors cultivate emancipatory hope in black teens? How can youth become revered leaders in the church? In this chapter I consider these questions in light of the key themes of the preceding chapters. I do not intend to provide a formula for emancipatory hope in light of the themes, but simply to outline the type of leadership that I feel is necessary for enabling African American adolescent youth to cultivate a healthy Christian spirituality.

In each chapter of this book, I first identify and analyze some of the central concerns among the teenagers that I interviewed. Then I offer a constructive response, addressing the identified issues and suggesting ways of nurturing emancipatory hope as an aspect of a healthy spirituality in black teens. Chapter 1 attempts to conceptualize emancipatory hope. In chapter 2, my analysis focuses on racism perpetuated through language. I discussed the ventriloquation of media culture among black youth — that is, youth speaking through the voice of media culture in social language. I described how such language is connected to meaning-making and how it can fracture the spirituality of a teenager. My constructive response builds upon Elisabeth's Schüssler Fiorenza's notion of oppositional imagination as a way of knowing. This means resistance to one's present dismal circumstance by envisioning alternatives to the situation. Chapter 3 examines the problem of colorism, which is internalized self-consciousness about skin color among African American and biracial and multiracial teenagers. I suggested that colorism causes teenagers shame regardless of how they identify themselves racially. I attempted to illustrate the triumph over shame through midrash on Jephthah and Mary the mother of Jesus. I concluded that the shame generated by colorism can be overcome by examining Edward Wimberly's idea of moving to self-worth and away from shame. Chapter 4 considers the problem of loyalty among girls in racially mixed groups. I discussed the preference that loyalty in relationships supersedes loyalty to a cause. I illustrated wholesome examples of fidelity in the life of Daisy Bates, an African American woman whose loyalty to her community promoted the fight for justice. Chapter 5 investigates the problem of racial profiling, a potentially lethal manifestation of racism experienced by African American teenage males. I argued for moral agency among black adolescent boys, which is the means of action by which one ascertains that which is good and right for himself and others. Moral agency involves practical ways of confronting racial profiling. Chapter 6 examines the rage of African American adolescents and constructs a response of anger as a positive emotion based on the idea of holy indignation. This means rage that is expressed in the presence of the congregation and empowered to work for transformation of domination.

The themes from each chapter promote emancipatory hope as African American adolescent spirituality. These themes of oppositional imagination as a way of knowing, self-worth, loyalty, moral agency, and holy rage can be understood as strategies that encourage black adolescents to expect that God will transform the sites of domination and that black youth will demonstrate a self-understanding that they are agents of God ushering in human equality. The themes are strategies for freedom from domination, strategies for emancipatory hope. These strategies are somewhat similar to those practiced by the African American slaves, who fostered, sustained, and transmitted cultural mechanisms that enabled them to cope with their chattelhood.[1] African American slaves were able to create another world, which was countercultural to the white-defined world, "complete with their own folklore, spirituals, and religious practices." These strategies for coping with slavery included tales, songs, and prayers.[2] They fostered hope for the African American slave in the midst of a despairing situation. Leadership for fostering emancipatory hope in African American adolescents must view oppositional imagination, self-worth, loyalty, moral agency, and holy rage not only as means for surviving the present state of racial domination, but also as strategies for action to bring in God's vision of liberating hope. Leadership, both that of youth and adults, needs defining before describing the nature of leadership for emancipatory hope.

Leadership as Transactional and Transformational

Josephine van Linden and Carl Fertman have shaped my understanding of leadership.[3] Although they focus on youth leadership, they suggest that the concept of leadership development can apply also to adults. In my summary of their idea, I will focus on the development of youth as leaders and the role of adults assisting in this process.

Leaders are "individuals [both adults and adolescents] who think for themselves, communicate their thoughts and feelings to others, and help others understand and act on their own beliefs; they influence others in an ethical and socially responsible way."[4] Leadership can be categorized as *transactional* and *transformational*.

Transactional leadership involves doing leadership tasks. Characteristics of transactional leadership include:

- Values problem and solution identification
- Makes decision — even if everyone has not been heard — in order to move forward
- Uses standards and principles as guides in decision making
- Develops the self to be a better decision maker for the group
- Gets things done
- Recognizes the importance of the product
- Takes charge (personal power)[5]

Transformational leadership is concerned about being a leader, empowering people to transform themselves and institutions around them. Characteristics of transformational leadership include:

- Values the participation and contribution of others
- Takes all viewpoints and advice into account before making a decision
- Considers individuals within their context and situations
- Uses individuals to test decisions
- Develops the self first to be a better contributor to the group
- Learns from experiences to generalize to "real life"
- Recognizes the importance of the process[6]

Transactional and transformational leadership are used together in discussing the three stages of adolescent leadership development. These stages are (1) awareness, the consciousness that one has leadership potential; (2) interaction, the activity by which skills in leadership are developed; and (3) mastery, the achievement of specific leadership skills and activities.[7]

Stage One: Awareness. Adults help youth become aware of their ability to lead when they help them make distinctions "between being and doing aspects of leadership, while also helping teens think about their own leadership styles."[8] Adults should help youth distinguish between doing leadership tasks and being instrumental in individual and institutional change, thereby leading youth into an understanding of transactional and transformational leadership. Adults should provide adolescents with concrete leadership information that is connected to the contexts of groups that are aspects of their lives. These groups include peers, schools, families, churches, and workplaces. "The primary task in Stage One is to recognize a young person's leadership potential and then prepare him to move to a higher level."[9]

Stage Two: Interaction. Adults help youth learn more about leadership. Youth are helped to hone their abilities to make decisions; "they become increasingly aware of the variety of choices possible in any given situation."[10] Adults help adolescents within the leadership development process to move forward, even though they sometimes regress to attitudes and behaviors of the first stage.[11]

Stage Three: Mastery. "Often, the ultimate level of leadership development is thought to be achieved when people, both adults and adolescents, assume formal leadership roles in organizations."[12] Adults should assist adolescents in being competent within the areas of life that are significant to them. "Stage Three leadership is about stepping forward and being seen. It is the gathering and focusing of energy that allows adolescents to step into a new role in one area of their lives."[13]

Indeed, the three stages of adolescent leadership development and adults' assistance in this process are related to fostering youth leadership for emancipatory hope. I am particularly drawn to van Linden and Fertman's concept of transformational leadership as "being." This correlates with adolescents' agency in partnership with God, dismantling domination. However, I recognize the author's point that both transactional and transformational leadership must work in conjunction with each other so that adolescents can experience wholesome leadership development.

Adult Leadership

In addition to their assistance in adolescent leadership development, such adults must have two characteristics for fostering emancipatory hope: *embodied hope* and commitment to *human flourishing*.

Embodied Hope

Embodied hope has been illustrated in the preceding chapters. In chapter 1, I attempted to illustrate embodied hope through the life of Fannie

Lou Hamer. In chapter 4, I suggested how Daisy Bates demonstrates loyalty to her community and, consequently, her loyalty to the cause of justice in Little Rock, Arkansas. Her life also illustrates embodied hope.

Men from the Civil Rights Movement, from grassroots communities as well as those known nationally, also have demonstrated embodied hope. Exemplars range from J. C. Fairley and Father Quinn, whom we met in the introduction, to Martin Luther King Jr., "the drum major for justice" in the struggle for civil rights. Vernon Dahmer, a grassroots civil rights leader from Hattiesburg, Mississippi, is another example of embodied hope. His commitment to voter registration in Mississippi resulted in his death from severe burns after the firebombing of his home by the White Knights of the Ku Klux Klan of Mississippi. Dahmer reiterated his support for black voting rights even while lying on his deathbed. Dahmer was committed to his family of seven children and his wife, Ellie. His burns from the firebombing of his home were the result of successfully getting all of his children and wife out of the burning house safely. Dahmer placed himself in harm's way so that his family might survive the fire. Along with being loyal to his family, he remained loyal to the struggle for freedom.

Vernon Dahmer demonstrated characteristics of embodied hope in his commitments to his vocation and to his family. Adult leaders who embody hope model wholesome spirituality, clarity in vocation, and fidelity in marriage.

Human Flourishing

Human flourishing for all people occurs when the covenantal relationships or promises between God, other people, and ourselves are functioning appropriately.[14] It is analogous to the flowering of a plant. A flower flourishes when the "properties that constitute its nature are developed to a high degree."[15] An orchid is the best it can be when the right nutrients, soil, climate, water, and sunshine come together so that the whole plant, inside and out, develops to the ultimate degree. The psalmist speaks of flourishing in this way: "The righteous flourish like the palm tree, and grow like a cedar in Lebanon" (Psalm 92:12). In the same way, there are properties central to human nature, and the development of these properties is what makes for human flourishing "and a good human life."[16] Human flourishing is a state of being in the world that is more than mere existence, but rather, experiencing a quality of life that results from "a pattern of strivings over a period of time."[17] Human flourishing does not happen overnight; it is a process that is nurtured over time, given the optimum conditions. It is our coming forth in the fullness of our God-given potential. Human flourishing is God's gracious gift to humankind. We do not earn this state of existence; it is ours at birth. It is yours right now.

Again, human flourishing for all people occurs when the covenantal relationships or promises between God, other people, and ourselves are working correctly. "From a Christian standpoint the whole of humanity is to be understood as one covenant community."[18] God has created all people to live in covenant with God, with one another, and with all living creatures regardless of their inability to think like humans. God's covenant is inclusive in that it affirms the value of all creatures as good and makes human beings responsible for their care. God's inclusive covenant changes the triangle of divine relationships to the rectangle of divine relationships when animals, birds, fish, trees, rivers — all of God's creations — are connected in covenantal relationship. This divine agreement was established though "God's act of covenanting, an expression of God's intention in creation declared in Jesus Christ."[19] Through Christ's incarnation of God's love we experience the covenantal relationship of God with all humanity and living creatures. The words of the greatest commandments exemplify this covenantal relationship: "[Jesus] said to them, 'You shall love the Lord your God with all your heart, and with all your soul, and with all your mind.' . . . 'You shall love your neighbor as yourself'" (Matthew 22:37–39). This love forges a covenantal relationship between God, other people, and ourselves that requires a certain quality for those relationships, placing the dignity and mutual participation of all people at the center of human relationships.

Our faithfulness to the covenantal relationship obligates us to act in ways that institute and maintain human flourishing for all people, especially for the poor, weak, and vulnerable. This is the practice of seeking justice, a Christian way of life that upholds the covenantal relationship between God, ourselves, and others whenever human flourishing is compromised.[20] Injustice hinders people from coming forth in the fullness of their God-given potential and breaks the divine covenant between God, others, and ourselves. These are situations and decisions that impede the flourishing of an individual or a group of people.

My discussion of human flourishing, preceded by my thoughts on embodied hope, helps to illuminate the leadership characteristics among adults who seek to foster emancipatory hope in teenagers. These adults strive to assure ministry with black youth for emancipatory hope.

Youth Leadership

Ministry for emancipatory hope "equips" youth alongside their adult leaders "for the work of ministry, for building up the body of Christ" (Ephesians 4:12), which is the ecclesial work of Christians, individually and collectively, living into their vocation.[21] Emancipatory hope prepares African American adolescents for leadership so that they practice critical consciousness and a critical agency in the midst of the hegemonic evils of racism, classism, and sexism. As leaders, African American adolescents serve humanity and live out their calling as Christians. Youth leadership includes pastoral care, mission, church administration, worship leading, and creating music.

For African American adolescents, leadership can be practiced in a variety of settings, both inside and outside the community of faith. Examples are youth leadership in the service of pastoral care,[22] youth-designed and youth-implemented mission projects, and youth involved in church administration. Beyond the church, youth might become involved in social movements, such as campaigns against sweatshops and for debt relief for two-thirds of the global community. African American youth leadership includes involvement in the worship traditions of the black church. Some black churches adopt the popular approach of "youth church," in which youth worship separately from adults with the full complement of teenage leadership except for the preacher, an adult who is affectionately called the "youth pastor" and perhaps is an ordained minister.

Worship leading includes black youth serving as musicians, liturgists, and ushers. A related style of ministry is "Youth Sunday," in which youth ministry is organized around one Sunday in the month when black teens provide leadership for the entire worshiping community. In *Black and White Styles of Youth Ministry,* William Myers describes the latter approach to black youth ministry based on his ethnographic research with Grace Church, a United Church of Christ congregation in Chicago.[23] Grace Church encourages its youth to take full responsibility for worship every fifth Sunday. This means that youth provide leadership through the choir, the liturgy, and the sermon. I have worshiped in this congregation on several occasions while living in the Chicago area. My observations of fifth-Sunday youth worship and regular adult-led worship at Grace Church help me describe leadership development with African American youth.

Efficacy, both individual and communal, is particularly evident in the fifth-Sunday youth Worship at Grace Church. Prior to the worship celebration, youth practice every aspect of worship, guided by their adult youth leaders. Music, Scripture reading, prayers, and the sermon are rehearsed weekly prior to the youth worship. It is the sermon that most significantly promotes efficacy with Grace's black youth. Myers describes the content of one of the youth sermons. My observation and experience of a youth sermon preached by a teenaged girl were quite similar to his. A quotation from Myers illustrates:

> On one such [fifth] Sunday a young woman named Roberta brought the message. Reflecting on the problems facing King Ahab and his need for good advice (1 Kings 21), this high school senior noted how King Ahab's four hundred resident prophets were employed as "permanent religious advisors." Roberta suggested that these advisors had "developed an agenda" to keep their privileged positions — "they told the King exactly what he wanted to hear." . . . She continued, "Here we have four hundred prophets, all worried about keeping their jobs, holding those influenced-producing long lunches, staying on the King's good side, and getting promoted; they had their own agenda." . . . She then warned, "We should beware of people who *have their own agendas.*" . . . Reflecting further, Roberta stated, for example: "Some of today's educators comprise a myopic minority, a group who have internalized a completely Euro-centric world view and who look on anything African with suspicion and disgust."
>
> "As students spending a great deal of their time in school," Roberta suggested, "we often hear this myopic minority asserting that everything European is of value while everything African is worthless. These teachers, while not the majority, are nonetheless like the teacher who told Malcolm X, when he was a young and a smart student, 'A nigger like you should study carpentry, not

law.' " . . . Roberta concluded: "Folk like Malcolm X's teacher muti-
late our mentality and pervert our personality. Either they don't
care, don't want to make waves, or are so brainwashed that they
believe the racist lies they perpetuate upon our youth. Whatever the
reason, they steal our education from us and turn us out of schools
ready to serve the needs of the military-industrial system. Beware,
Grace Church, of folk like these teachers — a myopic minority — who
have their own agendas."[24]

I quote this passage to illustrate the self-efficacy that Roberta develops
as a result of her experience, as preacher, of interpreting Scripture and
proclaiming the word of God. Also, in Roberta's sermon we see a retelling
of the militant faith tradition of Grace Church, a story that Roberta and
her community of faith understand as "being centered in a spirit-filled,
oppressed people, African Americans who survived, with God's help, by
caring for one another."[25] I have observed the retelling of Grace's story by
the senior pastor during other worship services and also beyond the walls
of the church in casual conversation with adult members. Also, youth
who participate in dance ministry or in liturgical dance each Sunday
experience self-efficacy beyond the fifth-Sunday worship.

Ministry for emancipatory hope that promotes the leadership of
black teens in worship is one example of youth leadership development.
Another example of youth leadership is that of creating music. Youth
have the capacity to construct creative and melodious music. Such music
can be theologically and biblically sound when capable adults guide
these young artists. This is illustrated in a song of hope and perseverance written in 2002 by Faith Griffin, an African American high school
student:

> O, no, I'm not gonna quit
> I'm pressing on, 'cause I'm gonna win this fight
> No weapon formed against me shall prosper
> Because I'm on the Lord's side
>
> Why be afraid?
> Why have fear?
> Why have doubt?
> Just trust Him, believe Him
> He will be your strength

> He will be your rock
> He will be your shelter, your protector
> I'm not gonna quit, no
> I'm gonna fight the good fight of faith
> Letting patience have her perfect work
> I'm just gonna wait, wait

Faith speaks of the forces of domination that are weapons against her. She declares that she will persist in the face of these obstacles because of her faith in God and God's presence in her life.

Faith's song has the potential for making a significant contribution to sacred music. Although the version presented here was created without the help of an adult like those who assisted Roberta at Grace Church, Faith's song has key elements that are rudimentary for a significant contribution to Christian music.

A Brief Word on Context

Ministry for emancipatory hope works optimally in the context of a Christian congregation that espouses a spiritual tradition of social justice. Robert Franklin defines the social justice tradition as one that "seeks public righteousness through community activism, political advocacy, and preaching."[26] He cites Dr. Martin Luther King Jr. and Dexter Avenue Baptist Church in Montgomery, Alabama, as examples of a pastor and congregation committed to social justice.

Additionally, Franklin suggests three types of pastoral leadership for the social witness of the African American church: (1) pragmatic accommodationism, (2) prophetic radicalism, and (3) redemptive nationalism. A leadership of pragmatic accommodationism will seek "social empowerment through peaceable means that are cooperative." A leadership of prophetic radicalism will "pursue uncompromisingly the [goal] of social justice . . . which involves radical restructuring of the free-market capitalist economy" in the North American context. A leadership of redemptive nationalism will "seek to establish a separate black nation in which the dignity and human rights of black people will be secure."[27]

Although Franklin emphasizes the nature of pastoral leadership for the social witness of African American churches, he does not describe the nature of lay leadership. Indeed, lay leadership, both youth and adult, for social witness in the black church is similar to that of pastoral leadership. The congregation needs laypeople of all ages who practice compromise and cooperation, radical activism, and nationalism.

When Does Hope Seem Hopeless?

Racism is a crucial issue for the African American adolescents who shared their stories with me. Ministry that cultivates emancipatory hope in African American adolescents attempts to dispel hopelessness in that area for them. Emancipatory hope seeks to foster a Christian spirituality in black youth whereby they expect the dismantling of economic, racial, social, and political injustice, and whereby they view themselves as agents of God, transforming the world into a just society — indeed, ushering in the reign of God.

Notes

1. Katie Cannon, "Surviving the Blight," in *Inheriting Our Mothers' Gardens: Feminist Theology in Third World Perspective,* ed. Letty M. Russell et al. (Louisville: Westminster Press, 1988), 84.

2. Ibid.

3. See Josephine A. van Linden and Carl I. Fertman, *Youth Leadership: A Guide to Understanding Leadership Development in Adolescents* (San Francisco: Jossey-Bass, 1998), 8–10.

4. Ibid., 17.

5. Ibid., 19.

6. Ibid., 18–19.

7. Ibid., 19.

8. Ibid., 74.

9. Ibid., 80.

10. Ibid., 95.

11. Ibid., 97.

12. Ibid., 107.

13. Ibid., 113.

14. For the concept of human flourishing I have resourced heavily several articles in *Social Philosophy and Policy* 2 (1999). These include Douglass B. Rasmussen, "Human Flourishing and the Appeal to Human Nature," 1–43; Thomas Hurka, "Three Faces of Flourishing," 44–71; Thomas E. Hill Jr., "Happiness and Human Flourishing in Kant's Ethics," 143–75; and Thomas W. Pogge, "Human Flourishing and Universal Justice," 333–61.

15. Hurka, "Three Faces of Flourishing," 44.

16. Ibid.

17. Hill, "Happiness and Human Flourishing," 144.

18. Joseph Allen, *Love and Conflict: A Covenantal Model of Christian Ethics* (1984; reprint, Lanham, Md.: University Press of America, 1995), 39.

19. Ibid.

20. I give an extensive discussion of human flourishing in my essay "Justice." See Evelyn L. Parker with Raymond Rivera, "Justice," in *Way to Live: Christian Practices for Teens,* ed. Dorothy C. Bass and Don C. Richter (Nashville: Upper Room Books, 2002).

21. See Charles M. Wood, *An Invitation to Theological Study* (Valley Forge, Pa.: Trinity Press International, 1994).

22. See Kenda Creasy Dean and Ron Foster, *Godbearing Life* (Nashville: Upper Room Books, 1999).

23. William R. Myers, *Black and White Styles of Youth Ministry* (New York: Pilgrim Press, 1991).

24. Ibid., 97–98.

25. Ibid., 98.

26. Robert Franklin, *Another Day's Journey: Black Churches Confronting the American Crisis* (Minneapolis: Fortress Press, 1997), 42.

27. Ibid., 44, 45, 47.

INDEX